The Power Of
Heart-Centered Leadership

Discover how to be a powerful and inspirational leader.

By

Ghislaine Florence Labelle

Dedications

To all the wonderful people I've had the honor and privilege of coaching throughout all of these years, and who have embraced their personal transformation as leaders of their teams and families. Thank you for the journey we've taken together. All of you, without exception, have contributed to my own growth and transformation.

Thank you to my life partner Émile and my children, Nancy, Emmanuel, and Marie-Claude, for being part of my life journey and for allowing me to develop essential qualities as a Heart-Centered and responsible Leader in my life, my family, and my community.

Table of contents

Introduction

After more than twenty years of supporting and coaching leaders from various spheres of the business world, I felt the need to contribute to the transformation of the dictatorial leadership style, which is now outdated and completely misaligned with the new planetary energy. Moreover, we are all witnessing and experiencing the results of this dysfunctional leadership in our world today.

Contrary to what many people think, today's leaders are looking for more meaning in what they do, knowing deep down that they are, in some way, disconnected from their core values and the wisdom of their hearts.

Many people are seeking a connection and balance between their mind and their heart. They realize that they are sometimes misaligned and unhappy because they know they have sold their souls to satisfy their need for prestige, monetary needs, and power.

Burnout & Depressions have reached staggering levels, not to mention the number of suicides and attempted suicides due to this disconnection of the soul from its true purpose.

This book aims to raise awareness among anyone currently in a leadership position of any kind, whether you are the president or prime minister of a country, a CEO, a team supervisor, or even a parent, your words, actions and decisions have consequences not only on your people, your organization, your employees or your children, but also on the Whole… all of humanity.

May this book help you discover the true power that lies within your heart and help you realize the importance of your mission as a leader. It is not by chance that you find yourself in such an important role; life has chosen you as a leader.

So it is time to take note of it and align yourself with this great responsibility in order to make a difference not only in your teams, your organizations and your families, but also in the whole world, so that we can, collectively, create a better world that will be a projection of our own inner transformation as a leader and responsible human being.

Chapter 1
Why Heart-Centered Leadership?

As a Leadership coach, I realize that my mission in the business world is to ignite the inner flame that resides in the heart of every leader or manager, so that their role is seen as a mission, not a job or a way to prove their superiority over others. We are all part of each other. They are called to realize that the members of their team are all projections of themselves, that all reflect what lives inside them, the good and the bad.

Leadership chooses us, not the other way around. My life journey allows me to see this clearly now. Accepting this as our life mission and purpose will enable us to truly embrace this mission and pursue the path that leads us to our own development, while contributing to the growth of each and every one of us. Accepting and becoming present to this great responsibility is essential because, as leaders, we are role models, fathers and mothers of families; our attitudes and behaviors send strong messages about what is considered acceptable or tolerable in our society.

If we look at the state of our current society, we see the glaring results of the dysfunctional leadership we have all been subjected to for millennia. This dominant and dictatorial leadership style has generated multiple wars, genocides, economic crises, corruption, crimes against humanity, environmental crises, and the list could go on and on.

Leaders on the verge of dementia have had a huge impact, and they have a great influence on the future of our planet.

We must look back to our history to learn about these ego-driven leaders who killed and massacred millions of men, women, and children for their own glory and personal triumph. Their thirst for power and their great need to dominate and conquer the world had and still has a tremendous impact on humanity. Entire civilizations were destroyed and vanished. The greed of these dysfunctional leaders, focused strictly on their own glory, with no regard for the collective or the environment, sowed and generated a world of fear, violence, poverty, environmental pollution, and mistrust. The aftereffects have been felt from generation to generation, and we all still suffer them in our world today.

Here are the ten most destructive leaders in our history:

Alexander the Great: 356-323 BC. AD

He conquered Greece, defeated the Persian Empire, and conquered all areas in Asia Minor (present-day Turkey), Egypt, and India.

Julius Caesar: 100-44 BC. AD

He conquered Gaul and added it to the Roman Empire (Western Europe). He was a powerful and cruel ruler.

Caesar Augustus: 63-14 BC AD

Octavian was born and was one of the greatest conquerors in history. By the time of his death, he had doubled his empire, but at what cost?

Attila the Hun: 434-453

He was formidable. A barbaric leader. He was spoken of as the scourge of God. He devastated the Roman Empire and dominated all of Europe.

Charlemagne: 742-814

Known as Charles the Great, his brother died under suspicious circumstances. He carried out numerous attacks in the name of Christianity and ordered the execution of a thousand people a day.

William the Conqueror: 1028-1087

Also called William the Bastard. He was the illegitimate son of Robert, Duke of Normandy.

He invaded England, killed his opponent, Harold, Earl of Wessex, who had been crowned king after King Edward's death, and successfully conquered all of Scotland and Wales.

Genghis Khan: 1162-1227

One of the greatest conquerors in history was born in Mongolia. As his powerful army grew, he recaptured what is now China, territories in Russia, Turkey, the Middle East, and Persia. The number of people he killed is unmatched by any other conqueror. The number of territories he conquered was four times greater than the number conquered by Alexander the Great.

Tamerlane: 1336-1406

Also known as Timur the Lame due to partial paralysis, he claimed to be a descendant of Genghis Khan. He attempted to recreate the Khan Empire using his core Islamic beliefs to build an army and take over parts of Asia, Africa, and Europe. His army killed over seventeen million people, or five percent (5%) of the world's population at the time, using religion as a motivator.

Napoleon Bonaparte: 1769-1821

He conquered Egypt. He established laws to reestablish the Catholic religion. He gained power over several territories in Europe. One of the greatest conquerors in history. He successfully dissolved the Roman Empire.

Adolf Hitler: 1889-1945

He created the Third Reich, a dictatorship to eliminate the Jewish population. He triggered World War II. Hitler took over almost all of North Africa and Europe. He killed five to six million Jews, which represented two-thirds of Europe's Jews, and about 40% of the world's Jews.

We can also remember the genocide in Armenia, April 1915 to July 1916, which cost the lives of approximately 1,200,000 Armenians, the genocide in Rwanda in July 1994 with nearly a million deaths, the genocide in Bosnia 1992-1995 with approximately 33,000 deaths, and this, without counting the war in Syria, Ukraine, Gaza, and all the terrorist attacks sowing violence, abominations and fear in our world today, killing thousands of people. With all of these insane wars and crimes against humanity, what have we learned?

* (https://fr.wikipedia.org)

They all used the same common power:

They ruled by sowing fear!

No leadership from the heart could create and manifest such a world, because the heart cannot motivate or inspire a being to commit such atrocities! How is it possible for a human being to commit such crimes? The answer is simple: this becomes possible when the Being is completely misaligned and disconnected from the heart, where love, the very source of life, resides.

The new Heart energy is taking its place; the old, dominant, and overwhelming leadership format is no longer acceptable. Moreover, this old format is stifling and not accepted by our young leaders of the new generation. The new Heart energy pushes and inspires us to rethink our approach as responsible leaders of a country, a team, or even a family, because we all play leadership roles in different forms.

The new quality of leadership cannot be transformed through the mind, but only through the opening of the heart and connection with the Higher consciousness, the source of all. Through this, we will be able to transform our families, our teams, our countries, and humanity.

When I began my career as a Leadership coach, over twenty years ago now, I declared that I wanted to contribute to the transformation of the business world one conversation at a time, one leader at a time. Now, I am inspired to write this book because I want to contribute by reaching out to several leaders at a time, several families at a time, and above all, in my own way, make a difference in this world. I chose to be part of the solution, and not the problem.

Even in nature, we witness the importance of leadership. Every herd or community in the animal Kingdom has a leader to lead them. This is essential for their survival.

On the other hand, whether it is the animal kingdom or the human being, the source of life chooses to express itself through those who have been chosen to play this important role. Also, to be a powerful leader requires being completely aligned with the source of life that resides in one's heart, to be well guided and make responsible choices that will bring benefits for all, whether for one's family, community, business, country or all of humanity.

Am I a leader?

We can see the qualities of a leader at a very young age. If you watch a group of children play, you'll see that they already have an easy time taking the reins: they tend to lead rather than be led.

As an entrepreneur, looking back, I already had leadership skills at a very young age. At home, having a mother with fragile health, I took on tasks such as making meals, cleaning, and taking care of the younger children and my mother. As a teenager, I was captain of the tambourines in a bugle corps, formed a dance group, and taught choreographies for the end-of-year show. As a young adult, I began a career as a secretary, eventually finding myself holding executive secretarial positions. I then began a career in sales, eventually becoming the director of marketing and sales for international companies. Then, I became an entrepreneur and owned two companies.

Leadership is often something that has been within us since our early childhood, pushing and inspiring us to move forward in that direction. Leadership is the very source of life that desires to express itself through us. If we allow it to take its place and express itself through the path of our heart, it will attract to us all the opportunities, occasions, people, and situations that will allow us to play this very important role in our lives and in the world.

Here are some examples of leaders and influential individuals, not necessarily in leadership positions, but who have had an extraordinary journey that has impacted, in some way, people, organizations, communities, and families. All have demonstrated that leadership is part of their life mission and purpose:

* Barack Obama

He represents the American Dream writ large. Not only was he raised by a single mother, but he also became the leader of the free world. He did so as a minority. He was the first African American president. Obama instantly inspired millions of people around the world. He was awarded the Nobel Peace Prize. There is no denying that he is an inspiring, influential individual and a man of heart.

Oprah Winfrey

Unlike many celebrities, the waves she makes tend to always be in support of humanitarian causes. Coming from a very humble background, she uses her story to prove that anyone can achieve their goals and dreams. As a Black woman, she is a clear inspiration to all African Americans and women, and her influence truly extends to all races, genders, and age groups.

Mohammed Nasheed

Originally from the Maldives, he is well-known to those who follow environmental issues closely. He served as president between 2008 and 2012, gaining this position after being imprisoned dozens of times for political reasons. During his tenure, he sought to make his small country completely carbon neutral. While working towards this goal, he inspired several leaders around the world. Since then, the concept of carbon neutrality has been taken more seriously than ever, and Nasheed's influence undoubtedly played a major role in this.

Bill Gates

Bill Gates has shattered the myth that billionaires aren't generous. As the founder of Microsoft, he has always been firmly committed to the foundation he founded with his wife and co-runs, The Bill and Melinda Gates Foundation, which works to improve education in the United States, combat infectious diseases, and combat poverty through global food supplies.

* (Top 10 Most Inspiring Leaders Today - College Degree Search - Google)

***Terry Fox**

By continuing his Marathon of Hope across Canada in 1980, Terry became a source of inspiration, courage, and influence, not only for all Canadians but also for the entire world. Having had one leg amputated following a diagnosis of bone cancer at the age of 18, this didn't stop him from beginning his Marathon of Hope, a cross-country journey to raise funds for cancer research. Although he was unable to complete the journey, the process made him a national hero, and more than $650 million was raised in his name. He was the youngest person to be awarded the Order of Canada in 1981, shortly before his death. The first Terry Fox Run took place approximately two months later.

Viola Desmond

She was the first Canadian woman to appear on our currency. She was a pioneer for Black rights in Nova Scotia. On November 8, 1946, Desmond went to the movies at *Roseland Theatre* in New Glasgow, and after purchasing her ticket, she sat in the lower section, the lounge near the screen. When the manager informed her that the seating area was reserved for white customers only, she refused to leave.

She was forcibly abducted, imprisoned, and fined for defying authority, but she continually fought the charges and was finally pardoned in 2010, 45 years after her death. Montreal named a street in her honor. A woman of heart and courage.

Nellie McClung

She won the right to vote for Manitoban women in 1916, making Manitoba the first province in Canada to do so. Writer, teacher, wife, and mother of five, Nellie McClung always fought for women's rights. Later in her career, she moved to Alberta, where she became a provincial member of parliament and later the first woman to sit on the board of directors of the CBC, as well as being part of the Canadian delegation.

* (Top 10 Most Influential Canadians - National Globalnews.ca)

*René Lévesque

René Lévesque began his career as a journalist at the CHNC radio station in New Carlisle when he was only 15 years old. During his student years in Quebec City, he worked as an announcer at CKCV and Radio-Canada. In December 1943, thanks to his fluency in French and English, he was recruited as a war correspondent by the *Office of War Information,* the American press service responsible for covering U.S. military operations in Europe. He was deeply affected by this war experience, especially the discovery of the Dachau concentration camp, which he could never forget.

On June 22, 1960, René Lévesque was elected in the riding of Montréal-Laurier under the banner of the Quebec Liberal Party led by Jean Lesage. His greatest achievement as a minister was the nationalization of hydroelectricity, an issue of the 1962 election campaign (Maîtres chez nous) that brought Jean Lesage's Liberal government back to power.

In January 1968, he published Option Québec, which was the origin of the political party that was created a few months later under the name Parti Québécois. On November 15, 1976, the Parti Québécois won the election with 41.4% of the vote. René Lévesque introduced major reforms, including the Political Party Financing Act and the Charter of the French Language. René Lévesque was a very influential man of heart and a man of the people.

* (Biography René-Lévesque Foundation - 2009-2017)

* Michelle Audette

Born in Newfoundland and Labrador to an Innu mother and a Quebec father, she is one of the activists who led a veritable crusade for a national inquiry into the 1,200 First Nations women who have disappeared or been murdered over the past 30 years. In August 2016, the perseverance of the former president of the Native Women's Association of Canada was rewarded when she was named one of the five commissioners tasked with shedding light on this scourge that has been ignored for too long.

Anaïs Barbeau-Lavalette

With the strength of having written one of the most significant novels of the year, *"La femme qui fuit"* (Grand Prix du livre de Montréal, Prix des libraires, Prix France-Québec, etc.), the writer, filmmaker, playwright, and mother of three young children had the time – and the empathy – to help Syrian refugees. After being made aware of this cause thanks to her role as spokesperson for the *World Press Photo event,* she decided, in collaboration with photographer

Guillaume Simoneau, to put together her own exhibition on Syrian refugee families in Montreal. What's more, she and her family even committed to sponsoring nine new Syrian arrivals: two parents and seven children! No wonder she earned, with her life partner Émile Proulx-Cloutier, the National Assembly medal for her social involvement.

(www.ellequebec.com/société/reportages/30-quebec-female-personalities-who-inspire-us)

***Lieutenant General Roméo Dallaire**

Roméo Dallaire is the founder of the Roméo Dallaire Foundation's Child Soldiers Initiative, a global partnership whose mission is to end the recruitment and use of child soldiers. A renowned advocate for human rights, particularly regarding child soldiers, veterans, and the prevention of mass atrocities, the general is a respected advisor to the government, in addition to being a UN advisor and a former Canadian senator.

His courage and leadership during his mission in Rwanda earned him the Meritorious Service Cross, the U.S. Legion of Merit, the Aegis Award for Genocide Prevention, and the affection and admiration of people around the world. His dedication to humanity throughout this mission has been well documented in films and books, including his own book, *Shake Hands with the Devil: The Failure of Humanity in Rwanda.*

*(www.romeodallaire.com)

The list of influential and kind-hearted leaders who have made or are currently making a difference in this world is long and could constitute a book in itself.

These leaders all used a powerful common force: LOVE!

The purpose of this exercise is for us all to become aware that this style of leadership—heart leadership—has always existed, and it always will. The difference is that it will become increasingly widespread and more powerful in the years to come, as humanity will no longer tolerate the lack of love and respect, nor the irresponsibility of dictatorial and self-centered leaders, focused on their own glory and thirst for power.

You only have to look at the present world news to see that many people are beginning to speak out despite the fear, choosing to stand up for a better world, a world of freedom, a world of respect for the rights and freedoms of all men, women and children, as well as for the protection of the environment and our planet, in order to ensure a better life for their children and grandchildren, as well as all generations to come.

Chapter 2
Ego Or Heart?

Listening to the heart

For our leadership to be expressed through the wisdom of the heart, it requires that we listen to our inner selves.

When I work with Leaders and we start by exploring their core values, a revelation always occurs to them: they are surprised to admit that they have never really thought about them.

They quickly realize how disconnected they are, not only from their core values, but also from their feelings, having been programmed by a society that has dictated to them that there is no room in the business world for emotions and the heart! Quite ridiculous, because emotions are part of our human experience and consist of alarm systems to make us realize that we are making good and bad choices, not only for ourselves, for our lives, but also for the quality of life of others. It is impossible to make bad choices, which are not aligned with the will of our heart, and feel good, just as it is impossible to make good choices, aligned with the heart, and feel bad! But this requires always being present to our feelings, through which our intuition and our heart communicate with us.

Unfortunately, many leaders have chosen, in order to cling to their position, to sacrifice some of their core values and completely disconnect from their heart and intuition, that little inner voice that inspires and guides them towards the right decisions.

This propels them into low vibrations, where fear becomes the master and leads their choices, where the ego, through the mind, dominates and takes control, resulting in dysfunctional choices and not necessarily good for their people, their teams, their employees, or even their children. It is certain that in the medium or long term, the mediocre results will reflect this lack of wisdom in their choices, because these did not have as their primary objective the well-being of all, but only their personal objectives, often motivated by fear, such as the fear of losing their job, or the fear of tarnishing their personal image as a leader.

Upholding our values and core beliefs takes courage. But when we do, it always yields powerful results. I remember being confronted with my values during a problem our production department had caused during the major launch of a new pharmaceutical product in the Latin American market. We were going to be seriously late with the delivery of the sachets needed for this launch. This was a major client that contributed significantly to our company's revenue.

During a conference call, the president and the director of operations kindly asked me to lie to my client. I will always remember that moment, and my silence, which lasted at least a good minute. The silence was so long for them that they asked me if I was still there! After that silence, during which I could clearly hear my inner voice, the wisdom of my heart, I chose to respect my core values of honesty, integrity, and commitment.

I then explained to them that there was no way I was going to lie to my client, that we had to agree on a different approach, and that, in any case, every lie always ends up getting found out. And that the day this came to our customers' ears, we would not only lose a major client, but also a major source of income and, above all, our reputation in the field.

Then it was their turn to remain silent for a considerable length of time. The president finally replied that I was right, that our best option was the truth, and that it would be better to work with our client to find a solution that would suit all parties involved.

The outcome of the conference call with this major client was very powerful and positive; the client came to our aid, and we implemented a solution that worked for both parties. In addition, we had earned the respect and trust of this client, who remained with us for many years afterward. The choice I made, to respect my values, also earned me the respect of the President and the Director of Operations, because they knew they could also trust me as a leader, that I would be honest and have integrity in all my business dealings.

I've seen too many leaders torn between their values and the pervasive, dysfunctional leadership in their companies. When we work on their core values, they quickly realize the cost is far too high, and they shouldn't be sacrificed for a position, salary, or promotion. Our values are non-negotiable, even if it often takes fierce and courageous conversations to enforce them. But the payoffs are many and always worth the joy.

When we respect who we are, including our core values, the results are definitely positive.

When we respect and choose ourselves, including our values, we align ourselves with our heart, we collaborate with our inner source, which orchestrates all opportunities, all possibilities. It guides all our choices, our thoughts, our words, and our actions. But, in order to benefit from all this, we must first listen to it and hear its messages, which come through our heart, and not through our mind.

I have made important choices in the past that made no logical sense, such as leaving a job that was not aligned with my values, with three children at home, my salary representing the main breadwinner for the family, no job ahead of me, while the economy was significantly slowed down, and the unemployment rate was high. Despite all these obstacles, and thanks to the guidance of my heart and the respect of my core values, I then found myself facing five job offers. I did not miss a single week of pay during the period when the interviews took place, and I made my choice. In fact, I worked for twelve years with the company I then chose, as the Company culture was aligned with my core values.

Here's another great example of a leader who didn't make choices inspired by his heart, but rather dictated by his ego. In fact, it's the story of the owner and CEO of the new company I had the great pleasure of working for twelve years as a sales manager. However, to respect anonymity, I'll use fictitious names.

The son of the owner and operations manager of this company, Brian, managed the production department from his ego. This company is a highly regarded manufacturing subcontractor in the cosmetics and pharmaceutical markets. His father, Doug, had built a very successful business from scratch. Doug was a recovered alcoholic who had taken charge of his life. I had a lot of respect for this man, with whom I truly enjoyed working.

Doug was a leader of heart. He was loved and respected by all the company's employees, many of whom had held their jobs for many years. When he walked through the factory, he always stopped to chat with the employees on the production lines. He greeted all employees by their first names and asked them about their children and families. When he saw new employees in the factory, he took the time to introduce himself to get to know them, and when he saw them again, he would greet them by their first names. In 2003, the company had 150 employees. Most of the team members had been with the organization for at least ten years or more. A key element of his company's vitality and prosperity was his humane and respectful management style. He also had the brilliant idea of hiring Lee, a young quality control manager who, over time, became the company's president. In fact, he used Lee as a buffer, a filter between himself and his own son, Brian, to ensure that his business was run in a healthy manner. Naturally, Lee was also a kind-hearted man, sharing the same values as Doug. Lee worked for the company for more than 40 years until it was sold.

Brian had to report to Lee, whose patience, tolerance, and perseverance I admired, because Brian regularly sought to sabotage the company's success and did everything in his power to cause unpleasant situations with the sales team as well as customers, whom he sometimes liked to hold hostage. Doug and Lee were highly regarded by all customers and employees. The success of this company and its reputation in the field were truly a reflection of the heart-centered leadership of these two individuals, who held key positions.

Dishonest customers, who didn't share the same values as the company's culture, did not remain customers for very long. It also goes without saying that customers who adhered to the company's culture and values were long-time customers and treated as good business partners.

Working with Brian, Doug's son, required a lot of energy, not only from the president but also from the entire sales team. His destructive attitude and behavior, stemming from ego-driven management, generated many stressful and unnecessary situations for the sales representatives and the entire management team. But our synergy and commitment to our customers, employees, and colleagues were so strong that Brian continually hit a concrete wall. On the other hand, Brian's reputation was well known in the industry, especially because suppliers did not like to deal with him at all. Being on the front line of component purchasing, as he was responsible for production, his father, Doug, had to intervene often to maintain harmonious relationships with our long-standing suppliers.

The big disappointment came when Doug, knowing he couldn't pass the company on to his son Brian, decided to sell. Unfortunately, he then strayed from his values and his heart, choosing money—the largest amount possible—for the company instead of finding the best possible buyer and thus protecting his longtime employees who had built the company with him and who had greatly contributed to its success through their commitment, expertise, and skills.

Lee, who was the current president, along with two former employees, who were pillars and geniuses behind production and operations, made him an offer to become a shareholder in the company, offering a fair amount. They would also have allowed him to remain CEO for as long as he wanted. However, this offer stipulated that his son Brian had to leave, which was in fact the only condition these three employees imposed on him.

Additionally, another family-owned business, our supplier at the time for printed components for over thirty years, which shared the same values and had a very similar culture to ours, also made him a very fair offer. But Doug was asking for far too much money compared to the company's true value, which already represented a very substantial amount.

He followed his mind, not his heart, and then a very tempting offer from an American corporation made him falter. Instead of choosing the best buyer for the potential well-being of his employees, customers, and long-time suppliers, he sacrificed all of that to get the biggest amount of money possible. His ego won the day. He then became a multimillionaire, forgetting all those who had allowed him to build such a profitable business and who had literally helped him make it a great success. The outcome was very disappointing.

First, since his son Brian was not part of the sale agreement, the American corporation that had become the owner immediately got rid of him. Doug, the former CEO, who was supposed to stay on for a year, was shown the door after only six months. Also, during the three years that followed, many long-time employees—including myself—left the company, no longer able to work there because of the culture that had become very unhealthy and dysfunctional. In fact, everything was now focused solely on profits, with no consideration for employees or customers.

It was well known that the new owners paid way too much for the companies they bought, as they didn't understand the packaging industry, being all financiers and accountants who only dealt with numbers, not human beings. And the fact that key employees had left the company resulted in a precipitous increase in employee turnover. Consequently, the new owners sold the company for a pittance. It was this family company, a long-time supplier who had tried to buy the company directly from Doug, that finally acquired the company, and for a much lower amount than their initial offer. This is sad because if Doug had followed his heart, I am convinced that he would have sold significant shares to the three key people and pillars of the original company, and that the long-time employees would have remained with the organization for many more years.

The impact of the ego-driven choice doesn't end there. Doug, the former owner, died about two years after selling his business. Before his death, he had lost the respect and friendship of his three key employees and pillars of his company, to whom he had given crumbs at the time of the sale. His son, Brian, then set up a select fishing camp with the money his father left him, which was a failure all around, because, of course, he ran this new business as always, based on his ego and with all his arrogance. He went bankrupt in less than three years and lost all the money he had inherited from his father.

The impact of Doug's choice, former owner and CEO, was enormous, as he died of a heart attack soon after he was asked to leave the Company.

These are just a few examples among many. No leader wins in the long run if he fails to find balance between his heart and his ego.

It is time for all leaders to wake up and take responsibility for the important role they have chosen to play, whether at the level of the people, society, a team, or even their own family as parents. All leaders can transform the world we currently live in simply by aligning themselves with their hearts. Acting first with one's heart will have an impact on all the hearts around them, which will, in turn, open and become sources of direction throughout the entire world, a world that will finally be transformed by this new style of leadership.

A new heaven and a new earth

"The collective human consciousness and life on our planet are intrinsically linked. The new heaven is the advent of a transformed state of human consciousness, the new Earth being its reflection in the physical world."

***- Eckhart Tolle, Author of A New Earth**

Do you want peace? Everyone wants peace. Do you feel that something inside you would rather be right than at peace?

All it takes to free yourself from the ego is to become aware of it, since ego and heart consciousness are two incompatible things. Only presence can free you from the ego, and you can only be present now… not yesterday, not tomorrow, not a month from now! Only presence can undo the past within you and thus transform your state of consciousness.

"Being "is the true and deep self. Can I feel my essential identity as consciousness itself? Or do I lose myself in events, the mind, the world?

** (New Earth, Eckhart Tolle, Éditions Ariane)*

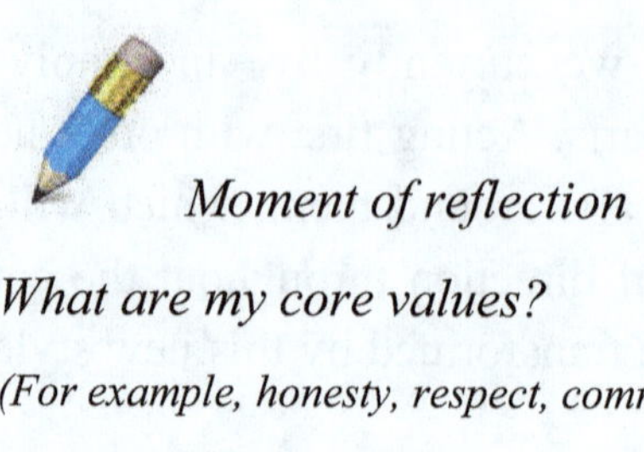

Moment of reflection

What are my core values?

(For example, honesty, respect, commitment, generosity)

____

____

____

____

Which of these values am I not respecting in my current situation?

(For example, honesty, respect for myself and my team)

____

____

____

____

What is the impact on my life, my work, my family life, and the management of my well-being of not having chosen to respect these fundamental values?

(For example, I feel unhappy, sad, stressed, and disrespected by some members of my team; I realize that I am disrespecting myself by sacrificing these values).

____

____

____

____

How can I honor and respect these values now? What benefits might I gain by respecting these values and honoring what my heart truly wants in my current situation?

(For example, by having transparent, respectful, and honest conversations with my teammates; by respecting myself; by no longer tolerating disrespect from my boss; by no longer lying to my teammates in order to support company decisions with which I truly disagree.)

____

____

____

____

What emotions are coming up right now just thinking about reestablishing my values in my life and in my current situation?

(For example, I feel at peace, I feel more powerful, freer, lighter.)

____

____

____

____

What specific actions do I commit to taking to restore these values in my life and in my current situation?

(For example, I will have good conversations with some of my team members whom I have disrespected in order to acknowledge my wrongdoing; I will have more honest conversations with my boss, during which I will affirm my values by letting my heart speak rather than my fears.)

____

____

____

____

The damage caused by the ego and forgetting "being."

* "The ego always identifies with the form, thus making you seek and lose yourself in one form or another" - "When every thought absorbs all your attention, when you are so identified with that voice, and with the emotions that accompany it, that you lose yourself in

every thought and every emotion, tell yourself that you are totally identified with the form and, therefore, under the influence of the ego."

***- Eckhart Tolle, Author of Nouvelle Terre, Éditions Ariane**

How many times, as a Leadership coach, have I been called upon to assist with cases of psychological harassment by managers who were driven by ego? Naturally, they themselves did not realize it, because, according to them, they were always right, and not the victims who had suffered the impact of their negative choices, words, and actions as a leader. On the other hand, their harmful and very destructive behaviors had a direct and significant impact on the lives of their victims.

Most of these Leaders weren't really aware of it until they embarked on a coaching journey, often imposed by their own Superior. When they find themselves with a psychological harassment case filed against them, their choice is usually to agree to undergo coaching to get help, in the hope of seeing a quick positive transformation in their behavior, or to leave their job at that company.

These interventions allow them to see and understand how they have not only made life miserable and difficult for some of their team members, coworkers, and those around them, but also the impact on their own lives and well-being by being completely disconnected from their hearts and core values.

An out-of-control ego can cause serious damage. Dysfunctional, abusive, overbearing, and often petty leadership is a glaring example of a power-hungry ego and its need to control others.

Unfortunately, this kind of leadership is the source of suicides, depressions, burnouts, separations, divorces, and broken families among the victims of this kind of abusive behavior.

Whether as a leader of a country, president of a company, father or mother, sports coach, or any other form of leadership, the impact of ego-driven behavior is always destructive, sometimes even bordering on insanity.

All the sexual harassment behaviors we hear about more and more in the media are examples of abuse of power and the ego's need for domination. The impacts are so devastating for the victims because they will never be the same again. The scars these people suffer will remain apparent throughout their lives. While many will be able to move on with their lives, these people will never forget the abuse inflicted on them by their tormentor. When a person in a position of authority exercises leadership from the heart, this type of behavior is inconceivable because the heart inspires them to want to care for and even protect their colleagues, teammates, children, and even an entire nation.

I experienced such a situation early in my coaching career with a Leader I will never forget and who left a lasting impression on me. I was then able to truly visualize a person who was experiencing an inner struggle between his heart (his soul) and his ego, which until then had had a very strong hold over him.

This individual, whom I'll give the fictitious first name of Henry, had previously worked as a consultant for various companies. He had been very successful in this role, which involved restructuring struggling businesses. Back then, Henry was doing what he truly loved, namely sweeping the floor and cleaning up corporate structures, including cutting jobs to make the companies more profitable.

Henry acted this way in Europe, Asia, and all over the world. He was very successful and managed to build a very good reputation for this kind of role.

One day, Henry partnered with a former colleague, Richard (fictitious name), and together they bought an advertising company, a field in which neither of them had any experience. This company had been wonderfully well-established in Quebec for a long time, with a very attractive clientele and turnover, in addition to counting among its clients some very important Canadian companies.

Henry and Richard took over the company, along with all its employees, some of whom had been working there for several years, including the vice-president of sales, Peter (fictitious name), who alone generated seventy percent of the company's revenue.

So Henry became the company's president, and Richard, the silent partner. In fact, Richard was simply an equal shareholder and consultant to Henry, as he also had another business that he had been managing for a long time. Over time, Richard became highly respected by all the employees, especially Peter, the Vice President of Sales, with whom he had built a very good relationship. Peter was a caring manager, honest, respectful, and committed to the well-being of employees, customers, and the company.

On the other hand, the company's president, Henry, wasted no time in getting into trouble. Being an ego-driven leader, and despite knowing nothing about this brand-new field, no experienced employee could, in his opinion, truly contribute to making the company successful. He had to be right at all costs, unlike the vice-president of sales, Peter, who respected all his customers and teammates.

Henry quickly became jealous of Peter, as everyone respected and believed in him. So Henry decided to make life difficult not only for Peter, but also for everyone who was close to him and supported him.

His petty and dictatorial behavior resulted in the loss of several good, experienced employees, who found new jobs with their biggest competitor. In addition, the company lost several major clients due to the fact that Henry had literally disrespected and disliked them, with his arrogance and haughty air.

Richard, who was seeing profits and revenue plummeting, called on my services to work with Peter, the Vice President of Sales, who was threatening to leave the company at the time, as well as with Henry, the President, whose behavior had been very unpleasant and devastating until then. Richard hoped that an intervention, through coaching, would calm egos and make collaboration between these two individuals possible, because the future and survival of the company depended on it.

After a preliminary assessment of the two individuals, as well as the sales team, I saw an opportunity to support these two individuals and the company so that it could grow by creating good team synergy, in addition to jointly determining clear and more motivating objectives for everyone. This represented a big challenge, but I truly believed in it. So, I confirmed to the silent partner, Richard, that it was possible to accomplish everything with work and perseverance. It was worth the joy of trying, because there was nothing to lose, everything to gain, since his investment was at risk.

After a very short time working with this team, I quickly witnessed the unhealthy dynamics of Henry and his out-of-control ego.

Peter, the sales team coach, had transformed himself considerably and had managed to gain the commitment of all the members of his team and build superb relationships with all of them, in contrast to the mistrust he sometimes received from them in the past.

Henry, on the other hand, who attended all the team meetings and also received individual coaching, had a lot of difficulty transforming his behavior, because the knowledge and tools he received during his coaching program generated a great internal struggle within him. Between our team meetings, which were nevertheless very positive and productive, he often worked hard to undo and discredit everything that had been put in place during the group meetings.

When I met Peter for his one-on-one meetings, he would share with me everything that had happened between sessions with the team, and often, I couldn't believe my ears. So, realizing that we would never get anywhere given Henry's continual sabotage, and after a long conversation with Richard, who had called on my services, we agreed that I could not continue this mandate without confronting, in a professional, respectful, but affirmative and direct manner, the president and his impulsive and negative behavior.

Just before confirming my meeting with Henry, I received a call from Peter, who told me about a situation that had just occurred. He was devastated and had made the firm decision to leave the company. He shared with me that he had resigned to Richard, but that Richard had asked him to wait a bit since a meeting he hoped would transform the current situation was about to take place with Henry.

On the other hand, what he shared with me really upset me, and I realized that Henry needed much more than coaching, having demonstrated a profound psychological imbalance! In fact, Peter shared with me that Henry had just had a crisis in his office and had smashed a wall with his fist, then went to the company parking lot, where he was seen in a crouching position (like a little man) screaming and crying like a child!

Most of the employees witnessed this completely dysfunctional behavior! Everyone was worried. So, I immediately advised Richard that Henry should be seen by a doctor as soon as possible to assess his physical and psychological state. However, my meeting with Henry was already confirmed, and I had committed to having a conversation with him, because he had been in a coaching program with me for several months, and had begun to open up and reveal very intimate things to me. He had nevertheless taken some steps in the right direction. He had honestly assessed some of his limitations and behaviors, and I had managed to gain his trust. He appreciated our conversations, although for my part, I admit that I often left our meetings feeling a little drained.

So, our meeting took place; we talked together for three hours. And on that occasion, I witnessed a spectacle that I will not soon forget. In fact, throughout our conversation, I remained in love and compassion, in heart and non-judgment, having promised myself beforehand to offer him a space where there is neither bad nor good, where there is only "what is". So, no judgment was made towards anything, in this blank space, free of everything, completely empty and meaningless.

I asked him with great love and compassion what had triggered this situation of despair he had recently experienced. And lo and behold, as he began to share the situation with me, I saw his eyes and every feature of his face continually transform before my eyes.

He literally transformed physically in front of me! I was so rooted in a place of love and compassion that I felt no fear. Sometimes his eyes and his entire face would resemble those of a reptile, and in the next few seconds, his eyes would become soft again and fill with tears. This back-and-forth in his face was truly impressive and reflected the inner battle between the heart and the ego!

My listening during this conversation, in a space of non-judgment, love, and compassion, gave him a space allowing him to express himself easily and to share his inner struggle with me. This interview lasted until, finally, his heart took over and he began to cry with relief, like a child. He then confessed to me that his father had abandoned him and his mother when he was very young and that they had lived in Europe, in near poverty. His father had not supported them financially at all, despite coming from a family that had a lot of money.

My client added that he had to work to pay for his own engineering studies. Later, his father, who wasn't getting any younger, approached him to help with his business, realizing he was the only one left to succeed him. He accepted his offer, taking great care to hide his intentions. Over time, he managed to gain his father's trust and eventually take over the company. His father then stepped back partially to let his son take over. And when Henry finally managed to take full charge of the company, he made sure to sabotage his father's business, causing it to go bankrupt. He destroyed everything his father had built over so many years. The damage had been done, and it was too late for his father to save his business.

He told me all this with great pride! Revenge achieved, yes, but at what a price! Through our long conversation, he realized that he was now sabotaging his own business because of his destructive behavior. He also didn't have a good relationship with his mother or anyone else. He had no empathy or compassion for anyone. His life partner, who was much younger than him, was literally afraid of him. Since their relationship wasn't born from the heart, neither of them could thrive in it.

He agreed to seek help because he was truly unhappy in every aspect of his life. When his heart, his whole being, and his conscience were able to take their respective places within him, he was able to distinguish that he was not his behavior, that this behavior came from something inside him that was taking control without his knowledge and making him say and do things that he was not proud of at all.

These types of behaviors are perfect examples of the hold the ego has over human beings.

I later learned that he had closed his company and returned to Asia as a consultant. I haven't heard from him since.

On the other hand, he really showed me the ugliness of the ego, literally physically. Today, when I share this or think about it, I still get chills! But this has taught me a lot, especially when I face leaders with behavioral problems. In such situations, I am now able to no longer see their behaviors, because thanks to love, combined with the creation of a space free from judgment, I instead find the light of the heart inside each of them. I then realize that by creating a space in which they feel comfortable expressing themselves, it allows them to discover this beautiful presence, this light, which lives within them. They can then see that they are not at all this machine that seeks to have a hold on them. They realize that they can make very different choices, coming from their heart, coming from love, and above all, out of respect for themselves and others.

We all witness, at one time or another, the results of harmful, ego-driven leadership in our world. Let us realize that this is negative and destructive, and can only generate suffering, violence, poverty, and the wars that we, as humanity, have suffered throughout our history.

Terrorism, the recent US elections, and corruption within governments are all results of ego-driven leadership and can only manifest in negative situations that have nothing to do with the well-being of each and every one. However, now that we are in a new era, that of heart opening and planetary ascension, nothing can remain hidden or secret. Everything is now subject to the light coming from our life source. As in nature, when light illuminates dark and gloomy areas, many vermin come out from under the rocks, from this place where they have sometimes been hiding for a very long time.

Chapter 3
The Dark Side Of Leadership

"We often perceive leadership as one of the elements that improves a team's effectiveness. However, this is to forget its dark side…"

*(Author: Malcom Higgs , The Dark Side of Leadership - Les Affaires.com)

So how do we sort things out?

By making the following distinctions:

- Create alliances with key people in the organization

- **versus**

- Using dishonest persuasion techniques.

- Persuade in a subtle and skillful way by presenting yourself humbly and with integrity

- **versus**

- Manipulate people and information.

- Allow yourself to have a global vision of any situation

- **versus**

- Controlling information to one's advantage.

How do you identify manipulators who are under the influence of ego?

Whether it's in your workplace, at home, in your social life, or elsewhere, you will always have someone who "gives you a hard time." It's important to understand that these people are not inherently "bad," but that these are simply mechanisms (mostly defense mechanisms) that they have developed over time, under the influence of the ego. You will have to "juggle" with these "manipulators" before they damage your team, your family, your communities... or even your enthusiasm and your joy of life!

*** Here are several examples of the typical "manipulator":**

- He makes others feel guilty in the name of family ties, friendship, love, and professional conscience.

- He shifts his responsibility onto others or shirks his own.

- He does not clearly communicate his requests, needs, feelings, and opinions, often responding vaguely.

- He changes his opinions, behaviors, and feelings depending on people or situations.

- He invokes logical reasons to disguise his demands.

- He makes others believe that they must be perfect, that they must never change their minds, that they must know everything, and respond immediately to requests and questions.

- He questions the qualities, competence, and personality of others.

- He criticizes without seeming to, devalues, and judges.

- He has his messages made by others.

- He sows discord and creates suspicion, thus dividing and conquering.

- He knows how to play the victim so that people feel sorry for him.

- He ignores requests made to him, even if he says he will take care of them.

- He uses the moral principles of others to satisfy his needs.

- He threatens in disguise or openly uses blackmail.

- He completely changes the subject during a conversation.

- He avoids or runs away from an interview or group meeting.

- He takes advantage of the ignorance of others and makes them believe in his superiority.

- He lies or preaches falsehood to know the truth.

- He is self-centered and can be jealous.

- He cannot stand criticism and denies the obvious.

- He disregards the rights, needs, and desires of others.

- He often waits until the last minute to order or make others act.

- His speech appears logical and coherent, while his attitudes testify to the opposite.

- He flatters to please, gives gifts, and suddenly starts taking great care of you.

- He produces a feeling of unease or unfreedom.

- He is perfectly effective in achieving his goals, but he does so at the expense of others.

- He makes us do things we would not have done of our own free will.

- He arranges himself to be the subject of all conversations, even when he is not present.

- *Excerpt from the book : « Les manipulateurs sont parmi nous »

- *Éditions de l'homme. Author: Isabelle Nazare-Aga

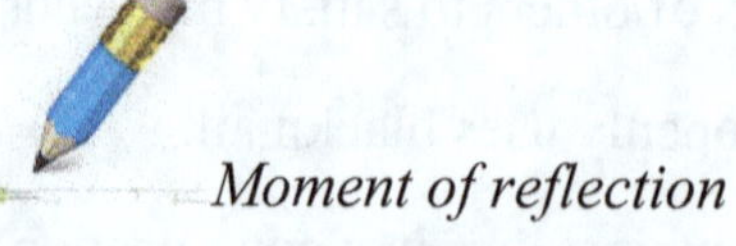 *Moment of reflection*

Take some time to think about the manipulative behaviors mentioned above and check off those you would like to be aware of so that you can avoid using them in your interactions with others in the future.

Here are some examples of leadership behaviors that come from our dark, ego-driven side:

- Abuse of power;

- Damage caused to others;

- Excessive control to satisfy personal needs;

- Circumventing the rules to serve one's own interests;

- Self-admiration;

- An excessive ambition;

- A tendency to see others as extensions of oneself;

- A tendency to be a profiteer ("I demand the respect I am due");

- Tendency to be bossy ("I like to be the center of attention");

- Tendency to be arrogant ("I am better than others").

The above-mentioned behaviors sow in others, whether in our countries, organizations, families, or communities, a discomfort that is fueled by fear and not by love.

When we slip into fear, we lose power and believe we are at the mercy of people, situations, or circumstances. Fear, a power that is the opposite of the greatest universal power, which is love, generates two "cancers" that we find in our world today:

1. The blame syndrome ("I must find and punish the culprit...")

2. Victim syndrome ("I'm at the mercy of... poor little me!")

The blame syndrome

Asking questions that begin with "who" and trying to blame others solves absolutely nothing!

These questions generate fear, destroy all creativity, and build concrete walls between our teammates, family members, and among different people.

Instead of brainstorming with the goal of working together, finding solutions, and getting things done, we "blamestorm" and accomplish absolutely nothing positive or constructive.

Have you ever wondered **"who they are"**?

They seem to be everywhere!

They must be a big, powerful group with a lot of influence because **they are** constantly being talked about!

Have any of you ever pointed **them out?**

For example, saying this:

-   That's **their** problem!

-   **They** have to do something to fix this!

- It's all **their** fault!

- They're **the ones who** ruined everything!

- **They** should know better!

Blame removes us completely from the equation, disempowers us, and prevents us from being part of the solution or creating solutions! We are all connected to each other, and one day, humanity will finally understand that what is done to one is also done to all.

By being aligned with our heart and with love, inspiration becomes accessible, where there are a multitude of solutions that we would never have thought of.

I invite you to do the little exercise below, very simple, but very revealing...

Who is to blame? (Complete each sentence.)

A poor teacher blames...	
A poor seller blames...	
A poor parent blames...	
A poor manager blames...	
A poor employee blames...	
A poor teenager blames...	
Someone responsible blames...	

If I transform my questions that begin with "who" **by using the following magic words,** at the beginning of each of my questions: **How can I? What can I do? How can we? What can we do?** I automatically activate my co-creative side and my proactive power.

I extract myself from fear to take back my power and become responsible. I thus automatically choose to be part of the solution, and not the problem.

Victim syndrome

Questions beginning with the words "why me?" and "why us?" come from people who suffer from the "PLOM disease.

PLOM = POOR LITTLE OLD ME! I am a victim of my environment and the people around me!

These aren't very productive questions, arc thcy? Yct, wc kccp asking ourselves these questions... We all fall into the trap of "why me?" or "why us?" from time to time.

Again, these reactions and behaviors come from fear, not from the power of love for self and others.

The solution lies in the magic words shared in the section on the blame syndrome. Choosing to be part of the solution, not the problem, whatever our role.

We are now entering a new era and a new global vibration, one in which the hearts of each and every person must begin to open. The awakening of hearts and the elevation of consciousness are necessary; human dissatisfaction with old forms of leadership based on fear and dictatorship is manifesting itself right now all over the planet.

We are all witnessing the current battle between these two vibrations: that of fear and that of the heart and love. This battle is simply a reflection of our own inner struggles. The more we open our hearts and give divine consciousness its rightful place, the more we will be able to be guided and inspired by it through our thoughts, choices, words, and actions. Then, the voice of our ego will weaken, and our mind will resume its rightful place: that of serving the divine within us, and not the other way around, as in the past.

I truly believe that the old form of leadership is coming to an end; I witness this during my coaching sessions. Each of the leaders with whom I have the great honor and privilege of working demonstrates their need for transformation, their dissatisfaction with the status quo, and their commitment to making a difference not only within their teams and their organizations, but also in their personal lives.

This is becoming increasingly evident with the new generation of leaders who are taking up more and more space, whether in the political, social, community or family spheres.

Leadership of the heart requires courage, faith, and a deep awareness. This leadership requires moving from unconsciousness to awareness, and this requires a healthy dose of humility.

When we are willing to accept that each member of our team, family, or otherwise is a projection of certain behaviors that need to be addressed within us as a leader, that we are truly all connected, and that when these unwanted behaviors are cleared and released from within ourselves, this inevitably results in a transformation on a collective level, even extending to the entire world. We then become much more aware and responsible. By taking the time to open and listen to our own hearts, we contribute to the opening of the heart of humanity.

There are no coincidences. Every member of our team, family, or community who attracts our attention with their disturbing behaviors did not arrive in our lives by accident. They are all actors projecting onto our screen what needs to be cleansed, purified, and released. Resisting this reality only brings repetitive projections, in different forms, which can only create and manifest the same results.

Suffering is the result of resistance; freedom is the result of acceptance. When we accept what is, without judging it, without condemning it, without labeling it based on our personal perceptions, we enter an empty space where we can receive inspiration for better choices, not only for ourselves, our team, or our family, but for all of humanity.

The more leaders in today's world raise their vibrations, live consciously, and open their hearts, the more we will all witness the new planetary energy taking its place, that of the planetary ascension that has already begun.

The conflict of the two energies, the two poles, negative and positive, is only a reflection of our own resistance and our own inner struggle; this new energy asks us to open our hearts and accept it to integrate it into our own lives.

Accepting and integrating this energy requires surrender and faith in our life source, knowing that our heart will guide us through our own ascension and transformation process. By not giving in to fear in the face of the significant change that is occurring, by not resisting it, everything will happen with much less pain and discomfort.

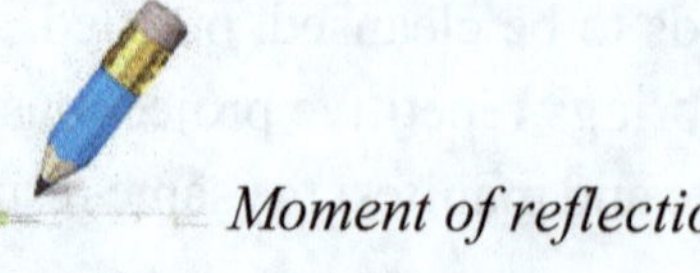 *Moment of reflection*

What behaviors are currently hindering me in my role as a leader (manager, parent, or other)?

____

____

____

____

____

If I let go of my fears and stop resisting the choices my heart inspires, what actions would be necessary to enable me to transform these unwanted behaviors?

____

____

____

____

By taking the actions listed above, what transformations and results do I anticipate?

We can no longer silence the light of our heart, which is increasingly taking its place, thanks to the consciousness awakening in each of us. This divine flame is eternal and cannot be extinguished. Our role is not only to let it take on all the place it deserves within us, but also to end our resistance so that it can fully expand as quickly as possible. By allowing our inner flame to shine, we automatically nourish the inner flames of all those we meet on our path. Moreover, when our radiant light, coming from our heart, expresses itself through us, souls are automatically drawn to us and come to warm themselves. The light is contagious and illuminates all that comes into contact with its presence.

A perfect example of the effect of this light comes from the testimonials of people who were recipients of it when they found themselves in the presence of Gandhi's wife. This woman's aura made anyone who was unpleasant become pleasant as soon as they found themselves within her energy field, which apparently extended for meters around her physical body.

How many people have also testified that when they were near Mother Teresa, and she made a request of them, it was impossible for them to refuse her anything.

Jesus is another great example. Everyone who came into presence experienced a profound inner transformation. And, even today, he leaves no one indifferent. The intense divine light that expressed itself through him manifested multiple miracles, and this light is still very much alive and active to this day.

There are also other great spiritual beings walking the Earth now who are manifesting wonderful miracles every day, but, naturally, our media does not talk about them. There are also many of them to whom the media does not have access because they work very quietly, in all humility, not wanting to become the stars that their egos would so much like to feed on.

If every person in a leadership position, at every level, commits to nurturing their inner light, it will quickly grow to the magnitude of a tsunami and envelop all of humanity and the entire planet.

We all have a choice about the type of leadership we want to demonstrate and how we want to contribute to the development of those around us and the world.

Chapter 4
Mobilization Through Heart Power

Great leaders of heart have generated wonderful results and thus transformed the quality of life of an entire people, thanks to their commitment to perseveringly following the inspiration of the Source of life within them.

Mahatma Gandhi was a great example of this. He was able to mobilize and inspire an entire people to follow him so that each of them would be treated with justice, respect, and honor. These people thus freed themselves from the British influence that oppressed them and prevented them from growing according to their own values and culture, also freeing themselves from a form of slavery and domination by the collective ego of their adversaries.

"The moment a slave decides that he will be a slave no more, his chains fall off." - *Mahatma Gandhi*

Nelson Mandela was also a persevering leader of heart who sacrificed more than twenty years of his life and kept faith in his vision and the divine inspiration within him, to free his people from the lack of respect and justice resulting, once again, from the domination and expression of the collective ego of his adversaries. Mandela succeeded in making the voice of the African people heard, thus condemning the grinding poverty, low wages, inhuman exploitation, and all the abusive policies resulting from white domination. **"All results of ego leadership."**

"The position of leadership was not historically bestowed upon certain individuals to be used or abused as they saw fit. Like all forms of leadership, it confers specific responsibilities on those who hold it."

- Nelson Mandela

Self-love is always reflected in how we love others. Dominant and overwhelming leadership simply reflects a lack of self-esteem and confidence. The need to feel that we dominate others is simply a result of the fear of being dominated. Lack of confidence in others simply reflects a lack of self-confidence. Whatever we do to others, we also do to ourselves. All these behaviors stem from our ego, and when our leadership is inspired by it, it is impossible to exercise powerful leadership in the long term, as the negative and destructive results will soon follow.

Love is the greatest force because it comes directly from our hearts. In fact, love IS our Source of life and our true nature. It unites, mobilizes, inspires, and literally creates miracles. The results generated by loving, heartfelt leadership are far more meaningful, powerful, and transformative, even propelling a people, team, or family beyond what anyone thought possible.

Divine love is comparable to the hub of a wheel: at the center of the wheel, everything becomes one. The further we move away from the hub of the wheel, that is, outward, the larger the spaces between the spokes become, creating the illusion that they are separate from one another. On the other hand, it is the center of the wheel that keeps everything in place and allows the wheel to be solid and whole. This is also the role of our heart: it is our center, our hub.

In the sacred center of our heart, we are all connected to life itself. In this center, we find peace and calm. Similar to the hub of the wheel, it is in this center that we become one with the Whole, with our creator and all of humanity. It is in our heart that we align with the Source of life and realize that we cannot be separated from it.

The heart has its own brain!

Did you know that the heart has its own brain? That it can function even without our mental brain. Yes, this has been scientifically proven. So, to make you aware of this great power that lives within us, allow me to share with you some scientific facts and discoveries:

***That the heart has a brain is a metaphor, right? NO.**

The heart has been found to contain **an independent and well-developed nervous system,** with over 40,000 neurons and a complex and dense network of neurotransmitters, proteins, and supporting cells.

Is it intelligent? Thanks to its elaborate circuitry, it seems that **the heart can make decisions and act independently of the brain** and that it can learn, remember, and even perceive. There are four types of connections that run from the heart to the brain. The heart's electromagnetic field is the most powerful of all the body's organs, being 5,000 times more intense than that of the brain. It has also been observed to vary depending on emotional state.

When we feel fear, frustration, or stress, it becomes chaotic. And does it reset with positive emotions? Yes. And we know that the heart's magnetic field extends two to four meters around the body, meaning that **everyone around us receives the energetic information contained in our heart.**

What conclusions do these discoveries lead us to? The heart's brain circuit is the first to process information, which then passes through the head's brain.

Could this new circuit be another step in human evolution? There are two types of heart rate variation: one is harmonious, with broad, regular waves, and takes this form when the person has positive, elevated, and generous emotions and thoughts. The other is disordered, with incoherent waves.

Does it appear with negative emotions? Yes, with fear, anger, or distrust. But there's more: brain waves are synchronized with these variations in heart rate, meaning the heart drives the head. The conclusion is that **love of the heart is not an emotion, it's a state of intelligent consciousness...**

And how can we activate this circuit? By cultivating our heart qualities: openness to others, listening, patience, cooperation, acceptance of differences, courage... And we do this 24 hours a day? It's the practice of positive thoughts and emotions. It's essentially about freeing ourselves from the spirit of separation and the three primary mechanisms: fear, desire, and instinct for domination, mechanisms deeply rooted in human beings, because they have helped us survive for millions of years. And how do we free ourselves from them? By adopting a witness position, by observing our thoughts and emotions without judging them, and by choosing the emotions that can make us feel good. We must learn to trust our intuition and recognize that the true origin of our emotional reactions is not in what happens outside, but in our interior. Yes! Let's cultivate silence, connect with nature, experience periods of solitude, meditate, contemplate, take care of our vibrational environment, work in groups, and live simply. And let's question our hearts when we don't know what to do.

* (http://www.vopus.org/fr/gnose/connaissance-gnostic/le-coeur-a-un-cerveau.html)

Heart leaders aren't just high-profile individuals; there are a multitude of quiet heart leaders we don't hear about in the newspapers and media. A heart leader is often recognized at their funeral, through the various testimonies recounting their life on Earth. As they make their way back to their life source, we become more aware of how many people have been touched by their presence, good deeds, and accomplishments.

I have several examples of unknown people who have accomplished things that might seem insignificant to our media, but who have had a significant impact on the lives of the people they encountered during their lifetime.

Among these leaders, some have saved lives through their care, love, and contribution, thus expressing their leadership from the heart.

For example, there's this man who, having lived through the Depression years, could never afford to go to college, a cherished dream. So he insisted that all four of his children go to college. In fact, his children often joked that the first words they learned to say were, "You're going to college." They all went. And even though their father didn't have a college education, he was still a math genius and got a top management position at TRW. He was even audited by the government because they couldn't understand how this man of limited means could have given away so much money in charity during his lifetime.

And although he retired after working forty-three years for the company, the role he played during all those years was barely mentioned during his funeral. However, it was his grandchildren who highlighted his role as a heartfelt leader by singing the song *"Did you ever know that you are my hero." His adopted son, who* lost his parents when he was very young, also joined them to sing. He was actually raised by his uncle and aunt, and then adopted by them when their own children were already teenagers.

His worth was assessed by considering his big heart, not the large monetary legacy he left behind.

Too often, we believe our worth will be measured by our appearance, our performance, our accomplishments, or even our assets. We set our life goals based on our wallets. We believe we are successful because we bought the nicest car, the biggest house, or our college degrees—all ego-driven needs.

The great value of this man was summed up in three points: his faith, his family, and his great contribution to those around him. His grandchildren also testified to this when they shared how the mark he left will never fade over time, especially his way of deeply touching people, not only his family members, but also his entire entourage and community.

So, as a leader, whether of a people, a team, or your family, what would you like to be the testimony of you when you leave this life? What would you like to hear? What imprint would you like to leave behind? Would it be profound, so that the years will never be able to erase it from the memory of the people you have met?

What will remain in everyone's memory will be a direct reflection of the kind of leadership you have expressed during your lifetime, namely, from the heart or from the ego.

Several years ago, a former mayor of a well-known city in the province of Quebec, Canada, was convicted and sent to prison after years of corruption and fraud. A man who was very well-known, very respected, until the light shone on the truth and the results of his ego-dominant leadership that lasted for more than twenty years. What was the impact of his choices, actions, and gestures, not only on the population of this city, who were exploited and outright robbed, but also on his family and himself? What will he leave behind? A sad result, a perfect example of leadership based on ego and not on the heart. The price paid for this kind of behavior was very high and not worth it! Yes, he was able to keep his throne for a long time, but not forever. Only love for one's neighbor is eternal and leaves a mark that makes a difference by contributing to the well-being of all.

Another example of leadership from the heart, from a well-known person, is Princess Diana. She was a member of the Royal Family, and the media harassed her constantly. She could have felt sorry for herself, but instead, she was able to exercise leadership from the heart by combining her popularity and the media to get humanity to join her in supporting great causes. So many gigantic fundraisers were organized by this great lady to help the most deprived. She made so many night visits to hospitals when she couldn't sleep, taking care to visit patients who were dying of AIDS or other serious illnesses.

We only had to watch her funeral, listen to the many testimonials of the people she touched, and witness the love her people had for her to understand the impact she had on the lives of so many. Her death saddened thousands of people.

"There is no difficulty that love cannot conquer, no disease that love cannot cure, no door that love cannot open. Rising high enough in love consciousness can solve everything. If only we could love enough, we would be the most powerful and happiest beings in the world." - **Emmet J. Fox.**

Chapter 5
The Inspiration And Wisdom Of The Heart Can Save The World!

Stanislov Yegrafovich Petrov was a lieutenant colonel in the Soviet army. On September 26, 1983, if this man had listened to his mind and logic instead of his inner voice, we would no longer be here, because all of humanity would have been destroyed by a nuclear war. That would have been the end of our existence on Earth.

More specifically, if this man had not been in office on the evening of September 26, 1983, and someone else had taken his place, the decision taken at that time could have been very different, generating devastating repercussions for the entire planet.

That evening, Petrov was at his command post. Suddenly, the alarm on their satellite computer system went off: a nuclear missile had just been launched in their direction, coming from North Dakota in the western United States. Immediately, the mandatory protocol in such a case was activated following Petrov's command. All ground systems, including the computer system reliability check, as well as all aerial satellites, were checked. All confirmed, except for the aerial visual verification system, that the missile had indeed been launched and was heading towards their country, Russia.

This event took place almost immediately after Russia mistakenly destroyed a private plane carrying hundreds of innocent civilian passengers during the Cold War. This action had just been condemned by the United States and President Reagan. This took place during a period when relations between Russia and the United States had become very tense. The Russians were already on high alert during this period, anticipating the possibility that the United States would take action against them. Therefore, a missile launch was, at that time, entirely plausible as far as they were concerned.

On the other hand, Petrov was not comfortable with the results and evidence confirming that this missile was on its way to his country because, after several minutes, the missile was still not visually captured by their satellites, which greatly bothered him. To everyone's surprise, the system gave a second alarm to the effect that a second missile was now being launched from the same location in the United States. Once again, a multitude of checks took place within a few minutes thanks to the computer system, which confirmed the veracity of this new information. Despite the fact that all eyes were on Petrov, not understanding why he did not sound the alarm and give the command to counterattack, he felt, deep down, that these missiles did not exist. He had no evidence to the contrary, apart from the lack of visual confirmation, which according to the experts on duty that evening, was due to the bad weather and the numerous clouds.

When a senior official called his emergency line, Petrov reassured him that it was a false alarm. However, his colleagues, discouraged and frustrated by his reaction and inactivity, could not act without his orders. They all disagreed with his inaction in the face of this emergency.

The system then indicated that a total of five missiles had been launched by the United States, and Petrov was certain that this could only be a problem with their computer satellite system, which was still quite new. He was convinced that the United States would not have needed to launch so many missiles at once.

Petrov's stress was at its peak as he listened to the inner voice of his intuition, his heart, knowing that the decision he made and the information he gave to those in high places would determine the future and continuity of our world as we knew it.

When his officers asked him, "What are we doing?" and while they expected his order to be to launch their own nuclear missiles, Petrov's response was, "We're not doing anything!" Everyone was in a state of shock, unable to believe their ears.

If Petrov had followed the pre-established protocol to the letter, if he had reacted with anger toward the United States, if he had made a decision motivated by ego and not by the heart, the order would surely have been given to launch their own nuclear missiles, which would have resulted in the end of our world. Many of us did not know that, on the evening of September 26, 1983, we all came very close to the end of the world, and that thanks to his divine intervention, this man saved us all from certain doom.

Petrov exercised leadership from the heart, defying all tangible and measurable evidence of their computer system, defying a protocol he was required to follow to the letter. His inner voice, that intuition that defied all logical evidence, guided him to a constructive decision that saved humanity.

Ultimately, it was proven that the system had indeed failed and that its false alarms had been the result of a rare alignment of sunlight and high-altitude clouds over North Dakota, on American soil, and the satellites ' Molniya orbits.

Petrov received no recognition from his own country. He was initially praised, only to be reprimanded by his superior commander for not having provided a full written report of the incident. This was made public with the publication of Yury's memoirs in the 1990s. Votintsev, who was the commander-in-chief when this incident took place at the *"Soviet Air Missiles Defense Units,"* came out. Following this publication, public interest in this previously unknown hero continued to grow.

Petrov received multiple recognitions, not only from the United States, but also from the UN and Germany. This very humble individual repeatedly repeated, during all the speeches he gave to various organizations, that he had simply been in the right place at the right time, and that he in no way considered himself a hero. Humility is always one of the behaviors that comes from the heart. He always insisted that his civilian training had served him well that evening and that another individual, who had simply followed his military training, would have made a completely different decision, which could have resulted in a nuclear war.

This is one more example of the impact and results of the kind of leadership we exercise while on Earth, as well as the legacy we will leave behind when we leave this Earth.

This man made his place in history and was recognized and honored for his bravery and courage.

Wikipedia, "The Man Who Saved the World",

https://web.archive.org/web/20110721000030/http://www.worldcitizens.org/petrov2.html)

The fundamentals of heart leadership

How do we know if we are living according to the principles and guidance of the heart?

- It requires conscious effort.

- It takes persistence.

- It takes courage.

- It requires a huge amount of commitment, and

- It takes a ton of discipline.

If only it were easy…

- If it were easy, we wouldn't need these principles and guidelines to be successful.

- If it were easy, it wouldn't be a challenge; and

- If it were easy, everyone would do them all the time!

Who among us doesn't feel the need to improve ourselves a little (or even a lot)?

- As a parent

- As a spouse

- As a friend

- As a partner

- As a citizen

- As a LEADER

Here are the five key principles that are an integral part of heart leadership.

Key Principle No. 1

- Words are worthless if actions don't back them up.

- We could change the world tomorrow if millions of people around the world acted on their true beliefs. **(Jane Goodall)**

Key Principle No. 2

- You are what you do!

- We appropriate a particular quality when we consistently act in a particular way.

- We become just by performing just actions, moderate by performing moderate actions, and brave by performing brave actions. (Aristotle)

Key Principle No. 3

- Everything you do has an impact, either positive or negative.

- Always act as if the whole world is watching you, because it always is!

- There is never a wrong time to do the right thing.

- It is impossible to be only 90% honest; you either are or you are not! **(Peter Scotese)**

Principle ^{No.} 4

- The golden rule remains golden.

- Treat others as you would like to be treated, and act toward others as you would like others to act toward you.

Principle ^{No.} 5

It's entirely a matter of character.

- C ommitment
- H onesty
- A ccountability
- Respect
- Attitude
- C ourage
- Trust
- Ethics & Integrity
- Responsibility

What type of leadership do I believe I am exercising, and what do I want to transform in my current situation?

____

____

____

____

____

What would I like to leave behind? What kinds of testimonials would I like to hear when I am no longer here?

____

____

____

____

What legacy, other than monetary, do I want to leave to my children, my family, my entourage and my community?

____

____

____

____

____

Chapter 6
How To Exercise Leadership From The Heart?

Leadership of the heart requires a good knowledge of oneself, recognizing not only our strengths, but also our true nature, which is divine.

Recognizing that we are all ideas and expressions of the Creator requires us to be aware of our power and to be responsible for it. Since we are all co-creators, we must be aware of what we desire to create and the impact our creations have on the Whole, on humanity. We must realize the power of our words, the tool with which all human beings create. Also, we must be aware of and responsible for all the words that come out of our mouths. As a leader, our words have a tremendous impact on the Whole. Besides, if I am not my words, I am nothing.

As quoted in the book: " **The Soul of Leadership** " by the great author **Deepak Chopra:**

"The words you speak are events. They have an effect on others, and you must never forget that. Your words develop your thinking, your emotions, your perceptions, your relationships, and your social role."

"Linguists say that speech isn't just about communicating ideas. A single sentence is multidimensional. Taking responsibility for your words means going beyond their content."

"Radiate your light as fully as possible. Keep the shadows to a minimum. Don't deliberately stir up ambivalence or unfathomable feelings." Express yourself coherently. Maintain courtesy and respect for others.

"Words are a window to the soul. You will achieve much more by opening it than by keeping it closed."

The manifestation of our creations should benefit everyone, not just ourselves. A highly regarded author and speaker I particularly appreciate, **Stephen R. Covey**, details in his bestseller * **"The Right Stuff to Lead"** published by **FIRST General Publishing,** the following fundamental principles as the basis of leadership.

Lifelong learning is fundamental

The principles are constantly enriched by reading, by following training courses, by listening to others, but above all by taking time every day with oneself in order to discover what our divine source has to share with us. This continual curiosity allows us to develop our skills, to increase our capacity to do things, and to guide us towards centers of interest that were previously unknown to us.

The inspiration to create extraordinary things comes from within us; we must spend time there regularly to tap into these creative ideas. How? By taking time every day to simply BE in silence, even if it's just fifteen minutes a day, to tap into this continual, limitless cascade of inspiration, where anything becomes possible. This inner connection is the basis of all leadership principles, regardless of level.

We also discover that the more we learn, the less we know! Knowledge is an energy that constantly renews itself. With leadership principles, you will develop your abilities more easily and quickly by learning to keep promises and commitments, not only to others but also to yourself.

<u>*Action:</u> I take time every day to remain in silence, listening to my heart and my inner voice. I am then guided towards the right readings, courses, and people who will help me grow and move forward in my life's journey.

Service at the heart of every mission

Those who base their lives on these principles see their lives as a mission, not a career.

Covey's metaphor that service, as a leader, is fundamental. He says it's like imagining yourself every morning putting on a harness and thinking about the work to be done that day. Imagine allowing someone else to adjust the yoke or harness throughout the day. Imagine yourself harnessed with another person at your side (a colleague or your spouse) and learning to move forward together.

We can think of it as a moral or intellectual exercise, but having a sense of responsibility and commitment to serve, as well as the desire to contribute, will be the only driving force that will allow us to move forward in the right direction, and much more quickly, without the feeling of heaviness of having to push or pull. Moreover, without the above elements, the attempt risks being in vain and exhausting us energetically.

***<u>Action</u>: I accept, in my life, the contribution of people around me who have the same desire to serve and make a difference in their world, whether at work, in their community, or at home.**

A perfect example of leadership that comes from ego, not heart, is often reflected in a great lack of accountability and respect for employees and the community. In 2016, a concerning and indecent situation was caused by the previous leaders in the Bombardier *organization,* due to their lack of empathy and consideration for their employees, as well as the Canadian people. At the that time, they had voted themselves huge salary increases after being financed and saved by the Canadian people themselves, therefore also by their own employees. This represents the type of results that ego and its insanity love to create.

No consideration for the fact that the company was saved from bankruptcy by the Canadian people, no consideration for the fact that they laid off thousands of employees in 2016, who contributed to their new salary increases.

***As quoted by Deepak Chopra in the book "The Soul of Leadership,"** the following eight points represent the responsibilities of a leader:

1. I am responsible for what I think.

    (My thoughts create my reality.)

2. I am responsible for what I feel.

    (My emotions and feelings confirm whether I am making the right choices).

3. I am responsible for how I perceive the world.

    (My beliefs generate my attitudes, my behaviors and my results.)

4. I am responsible for my relationships.

    (My surroundings are a good indicator of who I choose to be.)

5. I am responsible for my role in society.

    (Who I choose to be in the world impacts the Whole.)

6. I am responsible for my immediate environment.

    (I respect my environment by respecting myself.)

7. I am responsible for my words.

    (My words create, so I remain alert and aware of everything that comes out of my mouth. All my words must be aligned with my true intention.)

8. I am responsible for my body.

    (My body is a divine temple. I must treat it with respect. I realize that I need a healthy body to fulfill my responsibilities as a co-creator and leader.)

Positive energy

People who build their lives on these fundamental principles are joyful, pleasant, and happy. Their attitude is optimistic, positive, and radiant. Their spirit is enthusiastic, full of hope and confidence in the future. This positive energy is like an aura that surrounds them and transforms the negative energy fields around them. And when they encounter more negative radiation, they tend to neutralize or avoid it. Sometimes, they simply move away from the poisonous sphere. Wisdom gives them the sense of humor and appropriateness necessary to deal with it.

Be aware of your own energy and know how to control and radiate it. In a conflictual situation or one filled with negative energy, try to pacify the atmosphere, restore harmony to defuse destructive energy. You will thus discover how positive energy is transmitted, being particularly contagious when combined with trust and a clear intention aimed at the ideal solution for all parties concerned.

***<u>Action</u>: I remain positive and confident and focus on the best solutions for everyone.**

Mutual trust

This principle allows us to react with moderation and temperance to negative behavior, criticism, or human weaknesses. People who follow these principles are not surprised or threatened by the weakness of others; they are not naive, since they are aware of these human weaknesses. It is important to understand that there is an important distinction between behavior and "being" (divine potential) of a person. These two aspects are completely different. It is enough to believe in each person's own abilities. If we focus on each person's hidden potential (their divine being), it will be much easier for us to forgive and forget attacks or criticism.

We can also observe these behaviors as a projection of something that needs to be healed within us, or as situations or behaviors that offer us the opportunity to express strengths or qualities that have been dormant within us. By trusting that life sends us everything we need to mature and express our greatest potential as beings, it is much easier to see these people or situations as blessings and opportunities for inner transformation, instead of seeing them as threats. The more quickly we accept the life lessons they allow us to learn, the more quickly these people will leave our lives, or the relationship we have with them, regardless of the situation, will be completely transformed.

It is important to refuse to label, stereotype, categorize, or judge others. This requires constant awareness of our thoughts and beliefs, as it is so easy for us, as human beings, to fall into the trap of judging and condemning our fellow human beings, as we are all mean-making story machines!

People who apply these basic principles can already imagine an oak tree when they see an acorn and understand the process of helping the acorn grow into a large oak tree at its own pace. Their focus is on the potential (the oak tree), trusting that the oak tree is indeed present within the acorn itself.

Self-centered people believe they hold the key because of their superiority, that "thing" that sets them apart from others, but this can only be temporary. If you believe in the potential that lies within "us," not just within "you," if you are receptive, you encourage and allow this potential (the divine being) to express itself in all its splendor.

I'm not talking about people who continually abuse your trust and goodwill, and who behave dishonestly towards you or your loved ones. However, these people also have their reason for being in your life; very often, they find themselves on your path to teach you to respect yourself, to trust yourself, to assert yourself, and to honor your own divine potential.

***Action: I choose to remove my inner filters from my sometimes-erroneous beliefs and to look at others with the eyes of the heart.**

A balanced life

People who lead balanced lives read quality books and keep up with world events. They are socially active, have many friends, and a few confidants. They are intellectually and spiritually sharp and are interested in many things. One must read, watch, observe, and listen to learn. One must be physically active while having fun and enjoying themselves. A good sense of humor is essential, especially with oneself, and not at the expense of others.

We need a healthy and honest attitude toward ourselves. Our self-esteem must be manifested through courage, integrity, and modesty. The need to show off, to boast about famous relationships, to highlight our possessions, titles, or past successes are simply fruits of our ego, not of the divine being that dwells within our hearts. A need to prove oneself is directly linked to a need of the ego.

Leaders who want to uphold these principles must be open, simple, direct, and not manipulate others. They are not extremists— no "all or nothing"—dividing the world into right and wrong. They have the capacity to make good prevail. Their actions and attitudes are appropriate to the situation. They practice balance, temperance, moderation, and wisdom.

Good leaders are neither executioners, religious fanatics, political maniacs, nor dictators who violate anyone's rights and freedoms. They do not condemn themselves for their mistakes; on the contrary, they learn from them. They live meaningfully in the present and carefully plan, adapting flexibly when circumstances change. Their honesty is evident in their sense of humor, their ability to admit their mistakes, and their willingness to carry out their tasks with enthusiasm.

***Action: I stop taking myself too seriously. I assume my role as a leader with flexibility and lightness, with humor and joy. I play the game of life to the fullest, without fear of losing.**

Life as an adventure

It is important to savor every moment of life. Because serenity comes from within and not from without, it requires appreciation and beginning each day with a fresh and open mind, like courageous explorers who set out on expeditions to uncharted lands without knowing what awaits them, but convinced of their value in novelty and learning through experience. Rather than drawing on the resources of their usual comfort, in the security of what they have built, they find their serenity in initiative, creativity, willpower, courage, energy, and innate intelligence.

Seeing life as an adventure allows you to rediscover others with each encounter by asking them questions whose answers will foster engagement with them. These leaders know how to listen and benefit from exchange and sharing by demonstrating a genuine interest in others. They are not easily confused and seek to adapt to any unforeseen circumstances, two of their fundamental principles being flexibility and adaptability. They truly live fulfilled lives.

***Action: I open myself to receiving all the gifts available to me now. I express gratitude for all the beautiful blessings in my life, as well as in the lives of others.**

The Synergy

Synergy is the combination of several factors that contribute to an action, where the whole is greater than the sum of its parts. A person who lives by these principles is synergistic and becomes a catalyst for change. They can improve virtually any situation they find themselves in. They work hard and smart to be productive, but in a creative and constructive way.

A good leader will therefore have to harmoniously associate the members of his team by trying to compensate for the weaknesses of some with the strengths of others. To achieve the set objective, he will have to delegate his power easily and naturally by having confidence in his collaborators. No threat is perceived in the abilities of others, therefore no need for surveillance – or even spying – linked to jealousy. In the event of conflict, he will know how to keep his distance and dissociate people from the conflict or the problem that arises, by focusing on the interests and concerns of others rather than sticking to his positions. Together, we arrive at synergistic solutions that are, in general, much better than the original proposals, thanks to the compromise by which everyone gives and receives.

A powerful synergy occurs when everyone chooses to let go of the ego-driven desire to be right at all costs and is willing to hear and understand each other's perceptions and engage with a new shared perception that is beneficial to all.

***Action: I open myself to the perceptions of others, which may sometimes differ from my own. I am willing to listen to them and try to understand them with my heart. Together, we will create a new shared perception that will benefit everyone.**

Results from heart-centered leadership:

- Self-confidence;

- Perseverance;

- The medium and long term vision;

- Continuous motivation;

- Empathy;

- Compassion;

- Control and management of one's emotions; and

- Adaptability to people and situations.

Moment of reflection

Which of these fundamental principles challenge me? What actions can I take to implement and master them?

____

____

____

____

____

Chapter 7
Possible Transformations Through Heart-Centered Leadership

As mentioned in previous chapters, heart leadership requires presence and awareness. The more our leaders, parents, coaches, and all individuals open their hearts and raise their consciousness, the more the light of the heart will take its place on Earth, thus creating the New Earth we have been hearing about for decades.

This will require us to let go of the past, to choose to see our brothers and sisters with the eyes of our hearts, and not through the filters of our individual beliefs, prejudices, histories, and perceptions. These filters prevent us from truly seeing the potential of being within each person. This requires us to live in the "here and now," not in the past that no longer exists, nor in the future that does not yet exist.

Exercising leadership by remaining in the present moment allows us to enter a whole new space where the inspiration of the heart can communicate with everyone, without filters, without obstacles, without interference. Inspiration is necessary for creation, bringing extraordinary possibilities to our awareness and nourishing our imagination. Our imagination is the divine potential knocking at the door of our consciousness. Imagination, in turn, awakens within us an intense desire to act.

Let's take a moment to imagine together a planet that would be a direct reflection of the power of heart leadership, if all leaders in all countries of the world, and in all companies or organizations in the world, exercised, applied, and mastered this kind of leadership.

Let us take a moment to imagine together a planet if all leaders realized that they have nothing left to lose, that the pure and divine light coming from the heart will fill all needs, inspire the right thoughts, words and actions, and provide for all the needs of every human being on this earth, and not just a few selected countries or societies among many, but all!

Let's take a moment to imagine a planet together if all these leaders choose inspiration from the heart instead of that coming from ego and the fear of losing anything.

It is certain that a planetary transformation would result...!

I love John Lennon's song "Imagine," which is more appropriate than ever. If every human being took the time, every day, to visualize a planet completely transformed by the love of the heart, this vision would be created in the heart of each person. If everyone did this exercise daily, we could transform this planet at great speed, because our creative vision would be common, synergistic, and aligned, and therefore very powerful. But this requires commitment and the will of each individual. However, you can start now, individually, because your visualization will have an impact on all of humanity. It will be contagious because we are all one, we are all connected to each other via the Divine Source.

For anyone who has seen and enjoyed the movie "Avatar," you have most likely noticed that this wisdom is well demonstrated, especially when the tribe prays and repeats a mantra, each holding hands and all focusing on a common vision, a common intention. They listen to their spiritual master, who inspires them to pray, who guides them in this common vision, but this spiritual master realizes the need to draw on and mobilize the divine power within each member of his tribe so that the miracle can manifest.

We all have a great deal of inner power. Our current society reflects using this same power to serve the Ego, not the Source of Life or the heart. This same power, paired and aligned with the divine love within us, will be much stronger because love is the most powerful energy in the Universe. Until now, we have not been able to use it; we have allowed our Ego, our mind, and the opposite of love, which is fear, to take over, thus creating the world we live in. Of course, this is also a result of ignorance and false beliefs created by so-called spiritual leaders who have used their power and powerful influence to keep people ignorant, in fear of an imaginary God who crushes us and supposedly sees us as poor little sinners. This allowed these false leaders to better dominate and deprive human beings of their divine heritage, which consists of the power of creative love given to them by the Divine Source.

The need to dominate, crush, and keep humanity in fear is a behavior that results from the ego, which reflects our darker side.

On the other hand, consciousness is now awakening, the light of the heart makes us see clearly everything that was hidden inside each of us, so that we can cleanse, purify, and release our negative behaviors and replace them with those inspired by the heart.

I really like the metaphor described in the book "The Villa of Miracles" by the author Alain Williamson. In this book, the spiritual master gives his student a very meaningful experience by taking him on a sightseeing excursion aboard a submarine in the depths of the ocean in Maui. His guest then sees wonderful things, including fish with extraordinary colors and beautiful corals that cannot be seen on the surface of the water, but he also sees debris and waste. The spiritual guru explains to his student that this perfectly illustrates the elements of which we are unconscious, namely that there are very beautiful memories, very beautiful beliefs, but also debris and waste of which we are not at all aware. These harm us, being at the origin of certain attitudes and behaviors that do not serve us, nor do they serve the collective consciousness, humanity.

We must clear this emotional waste and debris in order to access divine consciousness and thus receive its messages and inspiration.

The Ho'oponopono method described in the book mentioned above, as well as in several other writings produced by various authors, dates back several centuries, originating more precisely from the ancient Hawaiian tribes, even before the arrival of Jesus Christ on Earth. A simple yet powerful method that allows us to clear our debris and waste in order to access a higher consciousness, the divine consciousness.

By using this very simple and detailed mantra in this book, by developing the reflex of repeating it regularly as soon as an aspect of ourselves needing to be cleansed is felt in our behavior or that of someone around us, by becoming more aware of the principle of necessary cleansing, we can quickly cleanse, purify and release the inner debris and waste that hinder our transformation, our ascension towards a higher consciousness, more aligned with our heart and with the Source.

The urgency of transformation is now being felt, and human beings know this deep down and are looking for solutions. More leaders are awakening, searching, and realizing that the old energy is no longer working. The more human beings awaken, which is already well underway and progressing, the more human beings will reject leaders who will not treat them with honor and respect and who will not have the well-being of all at heart. Not just their own people, but all peoples of the world. Then this New Earth will manifest through this new collective consciousness. This also applies to the environment and animals. New energy inspires and pushes us to evolve and experience transformation. It inspires and is the source of organizations seeking to uphold human, environmental, and wildlife rights, because all life is an expression of the Divine Source.

Eckhart Tolle mentions this very well in his book "*New Earth*" when he writes:

"Followers thus realize that the degree of spirituality has nothing to do with what you believe, but everything to do with your state of consciousness. And this state of consciousness determines how you act in the world and with others."

"But since the ego is destined to dissolve, all rigid structures, whether religious, institutional, corporate, or governmental, will disintegrate from within, no matter how deeply entrenched they may seem. It is the most rigid structures, the most impervious to change, that will collapse first."

" When we are faced with a radical crisis, when the old way of being in the world, of interacting with others and with nature no longer works, when survival is threatened by seemingly insurmountable problems, either a particular life form or species will die, or it will overcome the limits imposed on it and make an evolutionary leap."

We are witnessing that these prophecies are happening, that we are there, that the urgency of our transformation is now upon us. One only has to listen to the news to realize that this is manifesting. Our individual transformation will have an evolutionary effect on the Whole. This requires each of us to raise our consciousness. We are all leaders, we are all masters, so let us act this way in our lives, in our interactions with others, becoming responsible now for our thoughts, words, and actions. Let us be responsible for our creations, let us be committed, through our actions, to being models of this transformation. Let us inspire others to also want to raise their consciousness and thus access their divine potential.

I realize that I cannot control every situation, nor other people, but I do have control over one person, myself, and my reaction to the situations and behaviors of others. Raising my own consciousness allows me to be part of the solution and collective transformation, instead of contributing to collective problems. This requires being very present. Do I sometimes fall? Of course! But the difference lies in the fact that I have developed a reflex to clean up the mess and thus be able to bounce back more quickly. That is the difference. We each have great responsibilities: to transform our own behavior, to no longer play the victim and blame others, situations, or circumstances, to take charge and choose to create a better world, not only for ourselves, for our loved ones and families, but also for humanity as a whole.

This requires courage, perseverance, faith, and, above all, discipline to filter and choose what we will allow into our consciousness, as well as to stop acting like automatons, "beings" hypnotized by the illusion of a superficial world designed by the ego. It is very simple, a single fundamental law: "Anything that is not aligned with love and generated by love cannot come from the Divine Source." Moreover, anything that is not love cannot come from Divine Consciousness, nor even be part of it.

A leader aligned and inspired by the Divine Source cannot kill, crush, rape or destroy, not only his neighbor, but also his environment. A leader aligned with the Divine Source will have as his primary objective the preservation of life. A leader aligned with the Divine Source will have at heart the well-being of his people, of his children as a parent, of his team as a manager or coach, and will treat others with respect and honor, knowing that all represent a part of himself.

A significant portion of the Earth's population recognizes that humanity is currently facing a stark choice: evolve, transform, or die! A still relatively small, but constantly growing, percentage of humanity is in the process of breaking down old ego structures and entering a new dimension of consciousness. We are seeing more people overcoming their fears and taking to the streets to march courageously to challenge and say no to corruption, the abuse of power, and the lack of respect for human rights and freedoms.

"If the structures of the human mind remain as they are, we will always end up recreating fundamentally the same world, the same demons, the same dysfunction." - *Eckhart Tolle, "A New Earth."*

To add to this quote, not only will we reproduce the same dysfunction, but we will completely destroy our world. As I mentioned in a previous chapter, we came very close on September 26, 1983. A simple decision made differently, by an individual who would have been inspired by his mind (ego), and we would no longer exist today! The urgency to transform ourselves is obvious, if not, we will disappear from the planet, like the dinosaurs and several other civilizations.

On the other hand, a new energy is now available, a new vibration, and a New Earth. In the prophecies of the Bible, both in the Old Testament and the New Testament, the emergence of a "new heaven and a new earth" is cited. Heaven is not a place, but represents the inner realm of consciousness. This is the esoteric meaning of the term. It is also the meaning of the teachings of Jesus. The earth then becomes an outward manifestation of this inner heaven. Collective human consciousness and life on our planet are intrinsically linked.

"The new heaven is the advent of a transformed state of human consciousness, the new earth being its reflection in the physical world." *-Eckhart Tolle, A New Earth*

As mentioned by a multitude of authors, whether in matters of spirituality, esotericism, or prophecy, as the old consciousness dissolves, it is certain that, in parallel, geographical and climatic upheavals are occurring in many places on the planet, upheavals which we are already witnessing and which have greatly increased since the year 2000.

It is now necessary to act, to raise our consciousness, to become aware of the importance of each of our choices, and especially of our beliefs which no longer serve us, to replace them with those which are inspired by our heart and the Divine Source.

Moment of reflection

What am I now aware of because of this reading? What different choices can I make now? What transformations will become possible thanks to these new choices?

____

____

____

____

Chapter 8
Specific Actions To Awaken Our Consciousness

Meditation and silence

As mentioned in a previous chapter, we cannot raise our consciousness or receive divine messages or inspirations if we continually allow ourselves to be deafened by noise, social media, etc.

To raise our consciousness, it is necessary to take the time to BE, and stop DOING, even if it is only for thirty minutes a day. We are human "Beings" and not human "Doings"!

Find the best time of day that will allow you to develop and master your meditation sessions. Choose a time that will allow you to keep your commitment to your inner source and your heart. Since it generates everything, isn't it a priority to communicate with it regularly? What would become of your life as a couple if you never had time to devote to it? What if you stopped having regular conversations with your spouse? It's simple, after a while, it would be nonexistent. It's the same thing when we want to develop our communication with divine consciousness; it requires commitment, it requires our time. The more time you spend in silence with your inner Divine Source, the more you will elevate your consciousness.

When I go on two or three-day retreats of complete silence, people around me often ask me how I do it. How can you completely cut yourself off from the outside world and not get bored? My answer is always the same: "It's very easy for me, and I even fully enjoy these moments; it's a great gift, not a burden!" These moments of silence are important to me. Having a business that requires a lot of travel, and a career that requires me to be continually listening to others, I feel it when the time comes for me to take a good break and be in silence. My inner source, via my consciousness, calls out to me and asks for a meeting so that we can fully realign again.

During these stays, I don't listen to the radio or television, I don't use my computer, and I don't even visit social media. I remain completely alone with myself. All I have with me is a pad and a pencil, because I communicate a lot with my inner source through writing.

I'm often silent when I drive. I can easily drive from Montreal to Quebec City and back without a single sound in my car. This impresses my life partner, who hasn't been able to do it yet. I've also driven from Montreal to Kingston, Ontario, and back without a sound in my car. I love it! I particularly appreciate silence; it nourishes me, it inspires me, and it allows me to hear what my inner source wants to communicate to me.

When we experience true moments of silence, of inner listening (what I call meditation), when we take the time to develop these moments, to savor them, they become a fundamental need, and we can no longer do without them. When I began to meditate in 1984, I did it when my young children were in bed for the night, because during the day, I was caught up in the whirlwind of getting ready for work, getting them ready for daycare, etc. So, after bathing and tucking them in for the night, I would wait until they were deeply asleep, and this became my precious moment, my gift, my reward for the day. This moment lasted between thirty minutes and an hour, depending on my state, because I was sometimes more tired.

On the other hand, this meeting with my inner self had become the most important part of my day. These meditations allowed me to get through a very difficult time: divorce, being alone as a single parent with two very young children, financial difficulties, etc., and all this without sleeping pills or antidepressants. I managed to sleep well every night, unless one of my children was sick, which, as parents know, often meant having to pull a sleepless night. However, this happened very rarely.

These meditations raised my consciousness, brought me answers to problems and questions I was experiencing at that time, in addition to creating several miracles in my life. These moments of silence are now a fundamental need. My children are now adults and have left home, which allows me to meditate every morning. On the other hand, on days when I had to leave the house very early for business trips, the complete silence in my car while I drive still allows me to connect with my inner source, which is always with me anyway. This source being an integral part of us, it goes without saying that we are never separated from it. Any feeling of separation is pure illusion.

On the other hand, when my obligations demanded a lot of energy from me for a period of several months, the need arose for me to leave in silence for a few days, far from the outside world. As I expressed previously, during these periods of silence, I did not take any calls or emails; only silence, meditation, prayer and reading inspiring books were part of it, which nourished me and helped me, once again, to raise my consciousness.

Besides, my inner source always brings me, either through those around me or through the sharing of someone who has read a book, the spiritual education and personal development that I need. Isn't it well known that the books we are called to read always end up in our hands exactly when we need them!

The music

Music is a source of powerful vibrations that can quickly elevate our consciousness. Naturally, we must choose our music carefully not vibrations that create more stress, but those that relax us, calm the mind, and allow us to enter a space of peace and harmony.

Chanting also allows us to elevate our consciousness. In fact, some forms of meditation require chanting a mantra or simply listening to it being chanted. This also creates a vibration within us, making it easier for us to access consciousness, as the purpose of the mantra is to occupy the mind while we access a higher level of consciousness.

By the way, the *Ho'oponopono mantra* is available in both chant and music. I often use it as continuous background music in my car. This allows for continual inner cleansing, without our mind being able to intervene. The mantra does the cleaning work in our subconscious without us having to clear the inner debris through mental efforts that would otherwise be useless. I also sometimes play this same musical mantra as background music in my house while I do office work. I simply feel the inspiration to play this music from time to time, trusting my inner source that knows when I need it, when cleansing becomes necessary. I then invariably feel the difference quickly, almost instantly, dare I say. A feeling of pcace, calm, and clarity then takes place almost immediately.

One day, my cleaning lady, who also became a very good friend, suddenly started crying without knowing what was playing, and especially why she was crying. When she told me she found the music so beautiful, I shared with her what it represented and explained the reason for her tears. In fact, it was a sign that a part of her interior was being cleansed, purified, and liberated. She was impressed to feel what was happening, without knowing the reason.

One day, when I was on a business trip and we had several hours of driving to do, I played this music in my car while my work colleague and friend was also in the car. After a few minutes, she started to cry, without knowing why. I gave her the same explanation. Having read the book *"Zero Limits" by Dr. Joe Vitale, in which the Ho'oponopono* teachings are given, she understood what was happening and decided, too, to order the CD so that she could continue to benefit from it upon her return.

Among the gifts I received from the Divine Source was a good singing voice. So, I always sang in my youth, both at home and at school. I also participated in choirs.

On the other hand, when I went through a difficult period in my life, a long time ago, I had completely stopped singing, without realizing it, for several years. However, I listened to a lot of music and inspiring songs. One day, my life partner pointed this out to me, because he was used to hearing me sing in the car or while I was doing household chores. This made me realize that something was happening inside me, that I had buried and silenced part of my own expression. The difficult situations I had gone through had made me lose awareness of this gift that had been given to me, that of having a beautiful singing voice!

When I became aware of it again, I decided to practice a great song for my partner's sixtieth birthday, a song that represents us so well, " *Through the Years,* " a hit by country singer Kenny Rogers. So, without my partner knowing, I regularly met with my now deceased brother-in-law, a musician and singer, who had a lot of talent, and together we produced a soundtrack, because I was much too embarrassed, at that time, to sing in front of our family and friends at this surprise party I was organizing for him.

So, I had my brother-in-law record the music, which I then gave to my daughter, who came to film me practicing the song for my partner. They both did a wonderful job, and when the song and video were shown on a big screen for my partner and the guests, everyone shed tears, including me! At the end of that evening, many came up to me in shock, because no one, apart from my immediate family, knew I was singing. It makes me smile now, looking back at that moment from my past.

Yes, it was a beautiful gift to give to my husband, but the most important thing of all was to rekindle in me the desire to sing, because when I sing, it is therapeutic; my vibrations reach extraordinary levels, allowing me to feel alive and full of love. I then find myself in an indescribable vibration of love and joy. This event motivated me to take singing lessons, which became incredible moments of expression for me. And even if I sometimes arrived at my lessons drained and tired from my day, I left with energy through the ceiling! My partner was always impressed by seeing me come home with eyes sparkling with happiness and joy.

Singing once again elevated my consciousness, allowing me to reach inestimable levels of joy and enthusiasm. So, I continued my singing lessons for two years, with an extraordinary teacher who took me to a level I never thought I could reach.

Afterwards, my brother-in-law organized two fundraising evenings for Sainte-Justine Children's Hospital in Montreal, and he asked me to perform a few times in public, in front of about 150 guests. I was very nervous, but this experience made me aware that I was offering a gift to the audience, that I was sharing this extraordinary vibration with them, which gave me the courage to sing with great love and joy. I am always surrounded by music, whether at work, in the car, in the garden, etc.

Music is a fundamental element for raising consciousness.

At a jazz festival in Montreal, I experienced a moment of great presence as my husband and I sat on a restaurant terrace, very close to the main outdoor stage near Place des Arts. The music was playing, and I became hyperaware of the people—all from different age groups, different nationalities, different colors—following the rhythm with their heads, feet, and hands. Everyone was connected to the musical vibration of that moment, everyone was side by side, in peace and harmony. It made me see what would happen if everyone raised their own consciousness, thus raising the collective consciousness. We could, just like at that concert, all be close to each other, in joy, peace, love, and harmony. It's a matter of common vibration, of common consciousness.

Acceptance

Acceptance of what is, without prejudice, without judgment, without labels. Accepting differences is a very important factor, which allows us to let go of the resistance that only leads to pain and suffering.

The famous saying, *"What you resist, persists,"* is very meaningful. Acceptance allows us to make different choices in order to transform circumstances or situations. We cannot be guided by our inner Divine Source if we are busy putting all our energy into resistance. Resistance comes from fear, from ego, and becomes an obstacle to the guidance of consciousness.

The value of other people's perceptions

When we are aligned with divine consciousness and accept that we are all connected, all part of the Whole, it creates an opening to perceptions that may differ from our own. This gives us the opportunity to have a more holistic view of a situation.

When we realize that our perception of people or situations is generally mediated through our inner filters, beliefs, culture, background, and upbringing, it requires us to also realize that no one holds the ultimate truth, but rather that we all hold pieces of that truth. Only when we are willing to listen with the intention of truly understanding the other, and removing our inner filters, can we become aware of perceptions or solutions that were previously unavailable to us.

In my coaching sessions, I like to use metaphors and examples to help my participants understand the power of our internal filters and how they can color our perceptions of reality. I'm pleased to share one such example with you here.

Imagine your toddler starts elementary school and their best friend is named Patrick. They come home from school always talking about Patrick with excitement and joy. Patrick and I have done this and that together. You've even invited Patrick over to your house to meet him, and he really is a kind, friendly, polite, and well-mannered boy.

Recently, you were invited to a parent-teacher conference, giving you the opportunity to meet Patrick's mother for the first time. What perception do you have of his mother even before meeting her? Quite positive, isn't it? She must be a good mother since her son is such a nice boy!

Now, let's twist this story a bit. It's the beginning of the school year, and your son is facing the same Patrick, but this time, Patrick is the school's "Bully." He bullies your son, even going so far as to literally terrorize him. Your son has come home from school several times in tears, not wanting to go to school, and complaining of stomach aches. In short, he's not the same cheerful child you knew until now.

You're summoned to this same parent-teacher meeting, where you're meeting Patrick's mother for the first time. How do you perceive her now? How will you approach her about the situation your son is currently experiencing with her? You're already in a rather negative state, eager to put an end to this harassment. What emotions are you feeling now, anticipating this difficult conversation you have to have with this woman you don't yet know?

So, you see this lady, you approach her and you start the conversation by introducing yourself as your son's parent, immediately asking her if she is aware of the problems that exist between Patrick and your child.

She replied: *"I'm aware of this and I'm really sorry. You see, Patrick's dad just left our home, only a month ago, and Patrick is having a very hard time with it. Your son isn't the only one affected by his behavior, and I'm regularly called to meetings with my son in the school principal's office. However, we've sought psychological help and we're working hand in hand with the school administration to help Patrick get through this."*

How do you perceive Patrick's mother now? Haven't you moved from a rather negative perception, perhaps even tinged with a little judgment and condemnation, to one now tinged with compassion and understanding? Yes, and why? Because you've received a piece of truth and information that you didn't have at the beginning of your conversation. Now you have a broader, more holistic view of the situation.

I come from a printing background, where I learned early on that not all human beings perceive colors the same way, so why should situations and people be any different? Everything is colored by our filters. But when we are willing to truly listen to another person's perceptions, which differ from our own, we can then better understand why they may not necessarily see the same thing we do in a given situation. This requires us to put aside our filters in order to listen with the firm intention of truly understanding the other person and expressing empathy so that we see that same situation through their eyes, not our own. This requires us to let go of the desire to be right at all costs.

However, this does not necessarily mean that we will agree with the other person's perception, which differs from our own, but it will allow us to understand why this person might perceive this situation differently from us. The goal of the conversation is to create a solution together. To find a solution that is much higher than our own perception, a solution that will benefit all parties involved.

Know that your beliefs generate your attitudes, your attitudes generate your behaviors, which, in turn, generate your results. Your beliefs are not immutable, and by transforming them, you will automatically obtain new results!

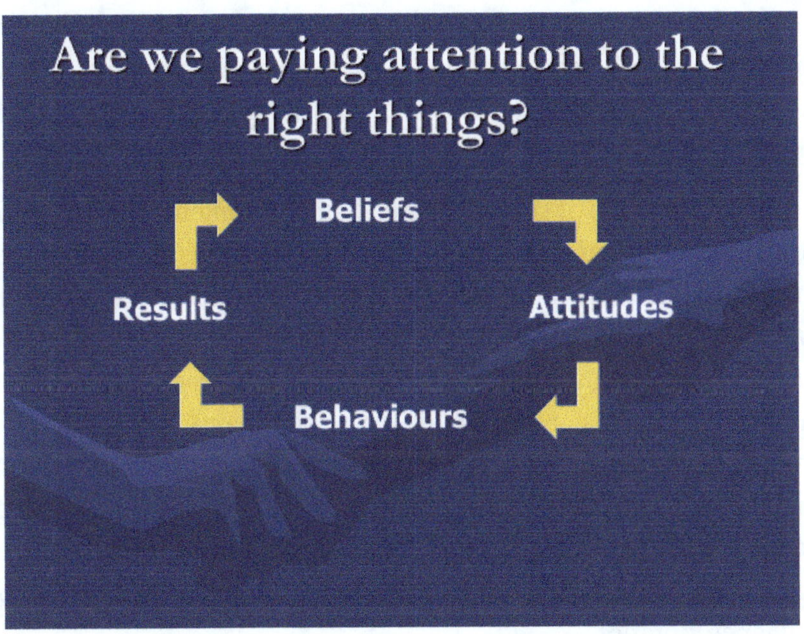

Are we paying attention to the right things?
Beliefs
Results
Attitudes
Behaviours

Creative power through the elevation of consciousness

If I can dream it, imagine it, perceive it, then I can create it!

As co-creators with the Divine Source, when we elevate our consciousness, this allows us to reach a state of imagination where anything becomes possible. As quoted in the Bible, Luke 18:27, " What is impossible with man is possible with God."

Whenever I need to recharge quickly, the best remedy for me is to go to the southern islands and spend some time by the sea. The mixture of sand, sea, blue sky, and dense vegetation filled with flowers and palm trees quickly elevates my consciousness and my energy field.

In my moments of solitude, when I stop to contemplate the ocean stretching out into infinity, I quickly manage to capture the immensity that lies within me. These moments allow me to visualize and believe in all sorts of wonderful possibilities. My vibration increases enormously and my creative side is reactivated. I enter another world, a completely different vibration, and I not only capture inspiring messages, but I also touch that part of me that vibrates with the Whole. I feel good, I feel at peace, in a form of ecstasy where I lack nothing. A space of great satisfaction and immense gratitude. The sea has always had this grandiose effect on my inner vibration.

As quoted by author Steven Covey, everything is created twice, once by the mind and the second time in the physical world. On the other hand, when the heart dictates and inspires our mind which, in turn, motivates us to act, then what we have imagined or dreamed takes form and manifests in the physical world.

All creation begins with an idea sown in our minds. But where does this idea, this seed, come from when we raise our consciousness? It is sown in our hearts by the Divine Source, which, in turn, inspires the mind to propel us toward action.

I love this quote, I read a long time ago in a Daily Word of Unity publication:

"The dream is simply God knocking at the door of your heart, informing you that your desire is already ready for you and simply asking you to be ready to receive it."

The inestimable power of imagination has been given to us by the Divine Source. We must therefore begin by imagining and visualizing what we desire, already seeing and feeling the end result of our creation, and then taking action to make it a reality in our physical world.

Every problem has a solution, and every goal or objective contains a divine plan for achieving it. For this to work, we must condition ourselves and anticipate positive outcomes. We must use our creative power, allowing our inner source to inspire and guide our every step. We must have absolute faith that we will receive everything we need to achieve our dream, at the right time and in perfect divine order. We must begin our creation by committing to our purpose, by positively anticipating it. This winning formula keeps us joyful and aligned with the inspiration and guidance of our heart.

As quoted in the Bible, Ephesians 2:10, *" For we are his workmanship, created in Christ Jesus for good works, which God prepared beforehand, that we should walk in them."*

Courage, an essential element in the practice of consciousness

When we raise our consciousness, we can never regress to being the person we were before. When we are disconnected from our inner source, we lack depth. Our world and our needs are superficial. We pay much more attention and put much more effort into looking good. We work hard to fit the mold dictated by today's society. When we live this way, in a state of unconsciousness, we believe we are the illusion our ego dictates, inevitably resulting in a state of constant dissatisfaction.

The best way to see that our ego is running the show is that we feel like we are "never enough" and that we "never have enough." There is always something wrong with ourselves or with others. We are constantly criticizing, judging, and condemning. We compare ourselves to others, and we compare everything to what the ego considers correct and normal.

Take my past for example. As a teenager and young adult, I was never thin enough, never beautiful enough, never competent enough. I continually compared myself to others. I was or had less than others, and this negative self-talk dragged on and on. Needless to say, I was miserable. My moments of true joy were few and far between, and they never lasted very long. These moments were temporary, as I believed that only situations or people outside of me could bring me joy and happiness.

During those years, my true happiness was therefore at the mercy of others. But one day, I realized that joy is a state of consciousness that results from a higher vibration that does not depend on circumstances outside of me. Joy, like love, is part of me. No one can take it away from me. I just need to raise my consciousness to be in this state.

Like many of you, before I realized this truth, I invested a lot of time and effort in doing whatever it took to fit into society's mold. I believed that my worth depended on other people's perceptions of me, as well as my accomplishments. My image was so important.

Once again, I will use a metaphor to illustrate this distinction.

Imagine you order a pepperoni and cheese pizza for delivery. Half an hour later, your doorbell rang. You open it and see the delivery person holding your pizza with his bare hands. The melted cheese is dripping a little over the edges of his hands! You ask him,

"Where's the pizza box?" To which the delivery person replies, *"Didn't you order this pizza?"* You reply, *"Yes! But where's the box?"* He then replies, *"The box costs a dollar more. Which is more important to you, your pizza or the box?"* You reply, *"The pizza, sure, but I value the box! This pizza is not acceptable without the box!"* The value comes from the dollar box, not from its contents, which is the part you'll eat, the pizza itself, which is more valuable!

It certainly wouldn't be hygienic to receive our pizza this way, but the principle is that we spend so much time and effort on our image that we forget the most important part, in which we should invest time and effort, namely our interior! Isn't it the most appetizing part! It is also the part of ourselves that can nourish others, because it is our interior that manifests on the outside, and this, according to our beliefs, our thoughts, our words, and our actions. We are not our outer shell, since our infinite value resides within us. Just like with the pizza box, the most important value is within.

Courage is a virtue that requires us to dare to be who we truly are inside, to have the courage to honor our own essence, our own truth, our own mission, and our reason for being. The courage to stop investing time, effort, and money in a shell that will die and return to dust! This does not mean, however, ignoring our physical and mental health, for we need our physical vehicle to create and live the life we were born to live. It simply means that it is necessary to have the courage to dare to be ourselves, to be authentic, and to offer humanity our own essence, our unique talents and gifts, and above all, to take responsibility for our own creations.

By raising our consciousness, we create from a state of love and joy. Our creations, which then manifest in the physical world, will automatically reflect our inner beauty, which will have nothing to do with our outer shell, our clothing, or our possessions. Rather, the radiance of our heart's light will be like a magnet, attracting to us beautiful people and situations that vibrate and are aligned with this same high frequency.

There are so many examples of leaders who have had the courage to challenge the status quo. Just think of Nelson Mandela, Martin Luther King, Malcolm X, Mother Teresa, Abraham Lincoln, Gandhi, René Lévesque, as well as many others who are lesser known but are part of our history. All of them contributed to raising the consciousness of our world today through their acts of bravery, courage, and perseverance. Their conscience drove them to contribute to something greater than themselves.

A great woman from Quebec, Thérèse Casgrain, advocated for numerous reforms in the 1920s, the most important of which was women's right to vote. In 1961, she founded the Quebec division of the *"Voice of Women" movement,* dedicated to world peace.

Our Canadian heroine, Laura Secord, who also risked her life during the war, was only recognized very late in life for her bravery and courage. Thanks to this woman who knew how to listen to her conscience and her heart, and not her head, she saved our country from the hands of the Americans. Many of us still don't know this great lady, whom many simply associate with chocolates!

Here is a summary of her courage, perseverance and bravery:

" Laura decided to go alone to warn Lieutenant FitzGibbon of the imminent American attack. She left before dawn and walked non-stop for eighteen hours, crossing farms, marshes, and forests, running the risk of being spotted by an American sentry. Almost at her destination, she met some native warriors and asked them to take her to FitzGibbon 's headquarters, to whom she conveyed her message.

Her efforts to warn the lieutenant were successful. The British forces and their Native allies, informed in time by Secord of the

American attack, were victorious. Had the Americans been victorious at Beaver Dams, they could have taken the entire Niagara region. Laura's contribution to this victory was kept secret since at the time the Secord family was living behind enemy lines and feared reprisals from American sympathizers living within the community.
Wikipedia

Here is also an excerpt from one of her letters that she sent to her close friend Mary, an excerpt that allows us to realize that there is still a lot of work to be done in our current world and that in many aspects, we have not yet raised our consciousness enough to transform certain situations which, in 2026, are still the same:

*"You have known me long enough to know that I share your opinions regarding the ambitions of man in general. Certainly, my humble opinion can easily be dispensed with in society, but I tend to believe that it is not tomorrow that men will start listening to women, who are much more peaceful. I am not clairvoyant, but I have to say that armed conflicts are not over **in this "low" world.** I have the impression, as you think, that the leaders of our country seek their little personal glory by means of great events that they provoke. But, beyond all these partisan quarrels, and at the risk of appearing contradictory to you, I understand the legitimate desire of man to fight for his freedom, to undo the chains that hinder him, to demand justice, and to desire peace of mind deep within himself. But humans are so weak that they sometimes forget their main reason for existing: love!*

Is it really any different in our world today? Do you agree with me that it is high time to transform our reality?

She was a quiet heroine, with no need to boost her ego through the recognition of her countrymen. She received recognition from the Prince of Wales at the age of eighty-five, until which time her act of bravery remained a secret, except for those close to her.

As quoted by Nelson Mandela: *"I can act as if I were brave, you know, as if I could beat the whole world. I learned that courage was not about not being afraid, but about overcoming it. I myself felt fear more times than I can remember, but I hid it behind a fearless mask. The courageous man is not he who does not feel fear, but he who tames it."*

Courage consists of:

- Follow your conscience instead of following the crowd;

- Refuse to engage in disrespectful and hurtful behavior;

- Sacrificing personal gain for the benefit of all;

- Authentically saying what you really think, even when others disagree;

- Take responsibility for all your actions… as well as your mistakes;

- Follow the fundamental principles and insist that others do the same;

- Challenging the status quo by seeking better solutions;

- Doing what you know is right, even if it involves risks and potentially consequences; and

- Stay aligned with your core values.

Conclusion

The dawn of creating a better world

As humanity, as co-creators, the Divine Source is pushing us more than ever to raise our consciousness in order to transform the world we have created until now.

Raising consciousness is each of our responsibilities. The more time and effort we devote to our own growth and spiritual awakening, the more we will contribute to raising collective consciousness and creating a better world together, a world without weapons, a world that respects and honors life in all its infinite forms.

We are all masters, and it is time we act like masters. We are all leaders, no matter what level we operate at. And as a leader, we also have the responsibility to wield this great power with love, compassion, and integrity, knowing that every thought, word, and action will have a direct impact on our future as humanity.

Seeing is not believing. Believing is seeing!

THANKS

My greatest wish is that this book can contribute to the various levels of leadership in our world today, whether leading a country, a team, or a family. In fact, my greatest hope, is that it will have contributed to the rising of the collective consciousness, and to the transformation of dysfunctional leadership styles, to "Heart-Centered Leadership". This will result in making a great difference in all of humanity.

Thank you to all the authors and teachers who have inspired me throughout my career to continually grow and improve, to remain aware of my beliefs, attitudes and behaviors, in order to become a leader who has made a difference in the lives of all the people I have had the honor and privilege of meeting, whether in my family, in my workplace, or in my community. A thousand thanks!

Thank you also to all my readers for your interest in these writings and for your encouragement. I am filled with gratitude.

Reading suggestions

New earth, Eckhart Tolle, Éditions Ariane

The Soul of Leadership, Unlocking your potential for Greatness Deepak Chopra, Harmony Books, A division of Random House

The Right Stuff to Lead, Stephen R. Covey, FIRST General Publishing

Thoughts for Myself, Nelson Mandela, Editions de la Martinière

Daily Word, Unity School of Christianity

King James Bible

The Villa of Miracles, Alain Williamson, Le Dauphin Blanc Editions

The Novel by Laura Secord, Richard Gougeau, Coup D'œil Éditions

Les Manipulateurs sont parmi Nous, Isabelle Nazare-Aga, Éditions de l'homme

www.ingramcontent.com/pod-product-compliance
Lightning Source LLC
Chambersburg PA
CBHW071454030726
47593CB00003B/999